Contents

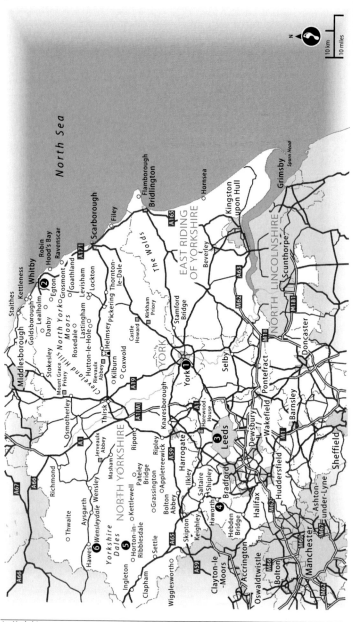

Filled with castles out of fairy tales and monuments to man's reverence for God, ruggedly beautiful Yorkshire is one of the richest regions of Britain for travellers. In the east, the rolling hills of the moors are thick with heather that turns the horizon pink in the summertime and nearly black in the winter. Here, villages like Lealholm make you stop in sheer wonder that something so perfectly pretty can exist in this modern age. The breathtaking views of the moors crashing into the sea on sheer cliffs that drop hundreds of feet to the icy waters is broken up by fishing villages like Whitby, with its gothic edge and homely centre, and little nooks like Robin Hood's Bay, with its smugglers' history and tiny cottages.

In the west, the craggy rocks of the dales seem to defy anything to grow upon their sharp edges, and yet the heather persists, against the odds. Here walkers follow trails to picturesque waterfalls, and then retreat to soak their feet in the fabled waters of gorgeous Harrogate. At the centre of it all, the soaring towers of York's historic cathedral is juxtaposed by the busy modern nightlife in Leeds and Sheffield, where the beat never stops.

Planning your trip

Best time to visit England

The weather in England is generally better between May and September, although it can be gloriously hot in April and cold and damp in August. The west of the country is milder and wetter than the east, whilst northern regions and mountainous areas such as the Peninnes are usually the coldest areas.

Transport in England

Compared to the rest of Western Europe, public transport in England can be expensive. Rail, in particular, is pricey compared to many other European countries. Coach travel is cheaper but much slower, and is further hampered by serious traffic problems around London, Manchester and Birmingham. Some areas, such as the Cotswolds, Peak or Lake District, are poorly served by public transport of any kind, and if you plan to spend much time in rural areas, it may be worth hiring a car, especially if you are travelling as a couple or group. A useful website for all national public transport information is **Traveline** ① *T0871-200 2233, www.traveline.info.*

Air

England is a small country, and air travel isn't strictly necessary to get around. However, with traffic a problem around the cities, some of the cheap fares offered by budget airlines may be very attractive. There are good connections between **London** and all the regional airports, although travel from region to region without coming through London is more difficult and expensive. Bear in mind the time and money it will take you to get to the airport (including check in times) when deciding whether flying is really going to be a better deal.

Airport information National Express operates a frequent service between London's main airports. **London Heathrow Airport** ① *16 miles west of London between junctions 3 and 4 on the M4, T0844-335 1801, www.heathrowairport.com,* is the world's busiest international airport and it has five terminals, so when leaving London, it's important to check which terminal to go to before setting out for the airport. To get into central London, the cheapest option is the London Underground Piccadilly Line (50 minutes). The fastest option is **Heathrow Express** ① *T0845-6001515, www.heathrowexpress.com,* taking 15-20 minutes. There is a train service **Heathrow Connect** ① *Heathrow T0845-748 4950, www.heathrow connect.com,* which takes 25 minutes. Coaches to destinations all over the country are run by **National Express** ① *T0871-781 8181, www.national express.com.* There are also buses to Oxford (www.oxfordbus.co.uk), to Reading for trains to Bristol and southwest England (www.railair.com), to Watford for trains to the north of England (www.greenline.co.uk) and to West London (www.tfl.gov.uk). A taxi to central London takes 1 hour and costs £45-£70.

   London Gatwick Airport ① *28 miles south of London, off junction 9 on the M23, T0844-892 03222, www.gatwickairport.com,* has two terminals, North and South, with all the usual facilities. To central London, there is the **Gatwick Express** ① *T0845-850 1530, www.gatwickexpress.com, from £17.75 single online,* which takes 30 minutes. **Thameslink** rail services run from King's Cross, Farringdon, Blackfriars and London Bridge stations. Contact **National Rail Enquiries** (T0845-748 4950, www.nationalrail.co.uk) for further information. **EasyBus** (www.easybus.co.uk) is the cheapest option, with prices at £9.99 single, taking just over an hour. A taxi takes a similar time and costs from around £60.

London City Airport ① *Royal Dock, 6 miles (15 mins' drive) east of the City of London, T020-7646 0000, www.londoncityairport.com.* Take the **Docklands Light Railway** (DLR) to Canning Town (7 minutes) for the **Jubilee line** or a connecting shuttle bus service. A taxi into central London will cost around £35.

London Luton Airport ① *30 miles north of central London, 2 miles off the M1 at junction 10, southeast of Luton, Beds, T01582-405100, www.london-luton.co.uk.* Regular **First Capital Connect** trains run to central London; a free shuttle bus service operates between the airport terminal and the station. **Green Line** (www.greenline.co.uk) coaches run to central London, as does **easyBus** (www.easybus.co.uk). **National Express** (www.nationalexpress.com) operate coaches to many destinations. A taxi takes 50 minutes, costing from £70.

Stansted Airport ① *35 miles northeast of London (near Cambridge) by junction 8 of the M11, T0844-335 1803, www.stanstedairport.com.* **Stansted Express** (T0845-600 7245, www.stanstedexpress.com) runs trains to London's Liverpool Street Station (45 minutes, £22.50 single). **EasyBus** (www.easybus.co.uk, from £2), **Terravision** (www.terravision.eu, £9) and **National Express** (www.nationalexpress.com, from £8.50) run to central London (55 minutes to East London, 1 hour 30 minutes to Victoria). A taxi to central London takes around an hour to 1 hour 30 minutes, depending on traffic, and costs around £99.

Manchester International Airport ① *at junction 5 of the M56, T0871-271 0711, www.manchesterairport.co.uk.* The airport is well-served by public transport, with trains to and from Manchester Piccadilly as well as direct and connecting services from all over the north of England. **National Express** (www.nationalexpress.com) runs routes covering the whole of the UK. A taxi into the city centre should cost around £20.

Birmingham International Airport (BHX) ① *8 miles east of the city centre at junction 6 on the M42, T0871-222 0072, www.birminghamairport.co.uk.* A taxi into the centre should cost from £25. Several trains per hour run the free 10-minute Air-Rail Link to Birmingham International Station, and other connections across England and Wales can be made by rail or coach, with **National Express** (www.nationalexpress.com).

Rail

National Rail Enquiries ⓘ *T08457-484950, www.nationalrail.co.uk*, are quick and courteous with information on rail services and fares but not always accurate, so double check. They can't book tickets but will provide you with the relevant telephone number. The website, www.thetrainline.co.uk, also shows prices clearly.

Railcards There are a variety of railcards which give discounts on fares for certain groups. Cards are valid for one year and most are available from main stations. You need two passport photos and proof of age or status. A Young Person's Railcard is for those aged 16-25 or full-time students aged 26+ in the UK. Costs £28 for one year and gives 33% discount on most train tickets and some other services (www.16-25railcard.co.uk). A Senior Citizen's Railcard is for those aged over 60, is the same price and offers the same discounts as a Young Person's Railcard (www.senior-railcard.co.uk). A Disabled Person's Railcard costs £20 and gives 33% discount to a disabled person and one other. Pick up an application form from stations and send it to Disabled Person's Railcard Office, PO Box 11631, Laurencekirk AB30 9AA. It may take up to 10 working days to be delivered, so apply in advance (www.disabledpersons-railcard.co.uk). A Family & Friends Railcard costs £28 and gives 33% discount on most tickets for up to four adults travelling together, and 60% discount for up to four children. It's available to buy online as well as in most stations.

Road

Bus and coach Travelling by bus takes longer than the train but is much cheaper. Road links between cities and major towns in England are excellent, but far less frequent in more remote rural areas, and a number of companies offer express coach services day and night. The main operator is **National Express** ⓘ *T08717-818178, www.national express.com*, which has a nationwide network with over 1000 destinations. Tickets can be bought at bus stations, from a huge number of agents throughout the country or online. Sample return fares if booked in advance: London to Manchester (4 hours 35 minutes) £28, London to Cambridge (2 hours 30 mins) £12. **Megabus** ⓘ *T0900-1600 900 (61p a min from BT landlines, calls from other networks may be higher), http://megabus.com*, is a cheaper alternative with a more limited service.

Full-time students, those aged under 25 or over 60 or those registered disabled, can buy a coach card for £10 which is valid for 1 year and gets you a 30% discount on all fares. Children normally travel for half price, but with a Family Card costing £16, two children travel free with two adults. Available to overseas passport holders, the Brit Xplorer Pass offers unlimited travel on all National Express buses. Passes cost from £79 for seven days, £139 for 14 days and £219 for its month-long Rolling Stone pass. They can be bought from major airports and bus terminals.

Car Travelling with your own private transport is the ideal way to explore the country, particularly in areas badly served by public transport. This allows you to cover a lot of ground in a short space of time and to reach remote places. The main disadvantages are rising fuel costs, parking and traffic congestion. The latter is particularly heavy on the M25 which encircles London, the M6 around Birmingham and the M62 around Manchester. The M4 and M5 motorways to the West Country can also become choked at weekends and bank holidays and the roads in Cornwall often resemble a glorified car park during the summer.

Motoring organizations can help with route planning, traffic advice, insurance and breakdown cover. The two main ones are: the **Automobile Association (AA)** ① T0800-085 2721, emergency number T0800-887766, www.theaa.com, which offers a year's breakdown cover starting at £38, and the **Royal Automobile Club (RAC)** ① T0844-273 4341, emergency number T08000-828282, www.rac.co.uk, which has a year's breakdown cover starting at £31.99. Both have cover for emergency assistance. You can still call the emergency numbers if you're not a member, but you'll have to a pay a large fee.

Vehicle hire
Car hire is expensive and the minimum you can expect to pay is around £100 per week for a small car. Always check and compare conditions, such as mileage limitations, excess payable in the case of an accident, etc. Small, local hire companies often offer better deals than the larger multinationals. Most companies prefer payment with a credit card – some insist on it – otherwise you'll have to leave a large deposit (£100 or more). You need to have had a full driver's licence for at least a year and to be aged between 21 (25 for some companies) and 70.

Bicycle
Cycling is a pleasant if slightly hazardous way to see the country. Although conditions for cyclists are improving, with a growing network of cycle lanes in cities, most other roads do not have designated cycle paths, and cyclists are not allowed on motorways. You can load your bike onto trains, though some restrictions apply during rush hour. See www.ctc.org.uk for information on routes, restrictions and facilities.

Where to stay in England

Accommodation can mean anything from being pampered to within an inch of your life in a country house spa hotel to glamping in a yurt. If you have the money, then the sky is very much the limit in terms of sheer splendour and excess. We have listed top class establishments in this book, with a bias towards those that offer that little bit extra in terms of character.

We have tried to give as broad a selection as possible to cater for all tastes and budgets but if you can't find what you're after, or if someone else has beaten you to the draw, then the tourist information centres (TICs) will help find accommodation for you. Some offices charge a small fee (usually £1) for booking a room, while others ask you to pay a deposit of 10% which is deducted from your first night's bill. Details of town and city TICs are given throughout the guide.

Accommodation will be your greatest expense, particularly if you are travelling on your own. Single rooms are usually more than the cost per person for a double room and sometimes cost the same as two people sharing a double room.

Hotels, guesthouses and B&Bs
Area tourist boards publish accommodation lists that include campsites, hostels, self-catering accommodation, hotels, guesthouses and bed and breakfasts (B&Bs). Places participating in the VisitEngland system will have a plaque displayed outside which shows their grading, determined by a number of stars ranging from one to five. These reflect the level of facilities,

Price codes

Where to stay

££££	over £160		**£££**	£90-160
££	£50-90		**£**	under £50

Prices include taxes and service charge, but not meals. They are based on a double room for one night in high season.

Restaurants

£££	over £30	**££**	£15-30	**£** under £15

Prices refer to the cost of a two-course meal for one person, without a drink.

as well as the quality of hospitality and service. However, do not assume that a B&B, guesthouse or hotel is no good because it is not listed by the tourist board. They simply don't want to pay to be included in the system, and some of them may offer better value.

Hotels At the top end of the scale there are some fabulously luxurious hotels, some in beautiful locations. Some are converted mansions or castles, and offer a chance to enjoy a taste of aristocratic grandeur and style. At the lower end of the scale, there is often little to choose between cheaper hotels and guesthouses or B&Bs. The latter often offer higher standards of comfort and a more personal service, but many smaller hotels are really just guesthouses, and are often family run and every bit as friendly. Rooms in most mid-range to expensive hotels almost always have bathrooms en suite. Many upmarket hotels offer excellent room-only deals in the low season. An efficient last-minute hotel booking service is www.laterooms.com, which specializes in weekend breaks. Also note that many hotels offer cheaper rates for online booking through agencies such as www.lastminute.com.

Guesthouses Guesthouses are often large, converted family homes with up to five or six rooms. They tend to be slightly more expensive than B&Bs, charging between £30 and £50 per person per night, and though they are often less personal, usually provide better facilities, such as en suite bathroom, TV in each room, free Wi-Fi and private parking. Many guesthouses offer evening meals, though this may have to be requested in advance.

Bed and breakfasts (B&Bs) B&Bs usually provide the cheapest private accommodation. At the bottom end of the scale you can get a bedroom in a private house, a shared bathroom and a huge cooked breakfast from around £25 per person per night. Small B&Bs may only have one or two rooms to let, so it's important to book in advance during the summer season. More upmarket B&Bs, some in handsome period houses, have en suite bathrooms, free Wi-Fi and TVs in each room and usually charge from £35 per person per night.

Hostels

For those travelling on a tight budget, there is a network of hostels offering cheap accommodation in major cities, national parks and other areas of beauty, run by the **Youth Hostel Association (YHA)** ① *T01629-592600, or customer services T0800-0191 700, +44-1629 592700 from outside the UK, www.yha.org.uk.* Membership costs from £14.35 a year and a bed in a dormitory costs from £15 to £25 a night. They offer bunk-bed accommodation in single-sex dormitories or smaller rooms, as well as family rooms, kitchen and laundry facilities. Though some rural hostels are still strict on discipline and impose a 2300 curfew, those in larger towns and cities tend to be more relaxed and doors are closed as late as 0200. Some larger hostels provide breakfasts for around £2.50 and three-course evening meals for £4-5. You should always phone ahead, as many hostels are closed during the day and phone numbers are listed in this guide. Advance booking is recommended at all times, particularly from May to September and on public holidays. Many hostels are closed during the winter. Youth hostel members are entitled to various discounts, including tourist attractions and travel. The YHA also offer budget self-catering bunkhouses with mostly dorm accommodation and some family rooms, which are in more rural locations. Camping barns, camping pods and camping are other options offered by the YHA; see the website for details.

Details of most independent hostels can be found in the *Independent Hostel Guide* (T01629-580427, www.independenthostelguide.co.uk). Independent hostels tend to be more laid-back, with fewer rules and no curfew, and no membership is required. They all have dorms, hot showers and self-catering kitchens, and some have family and double rooms. Some include continental breakfast, or offer cheap breakfasts.

Self-catering accommodation
There are lots of different types of accommodation to choose from, to suit all budgets, ranging from luxury lodges, castles and lighthouses to basic cottages. Expect to pay at least £200-400 per week for a two-bedroom cottage in the winter, rising to £400-1000 in the high season, or more if it's a particularly nice place. A good source of Information on self-catering accommodation is the VisitEngland website, www.visitengland.com, and its *VisitEngland Self-catering 2013* guide, which lists many properties and is available to buy from any tourist office and many bookshops, but there are also dozens of excellent websites to browse. Amongst the best websites are: www.cottages4you.co.uk, www.ruralretreats.co.uk and www.ownersdirect.co.uk If you want to tickle a trout or feed a pet lamb, **Farm Stay UK** (www.farmstay.co.uk) offer over a thousand good value rural places to stay around England, all clearly listed on a clickable map.

More interesting places to stay are offered by the **Landmark Trust** ⓘ *T01628-825925, www.landmarktrust.org.uk*, who rent out renovated historic landmark buildings, from atmospheric castles to cottages, and the **National Trust** ⓘ *T0844-800 2070, www.national trustcottages.co.uk*, who provide a wide variety of different accommodation on their estates. A reputable agent for self-catering cottages is **English Country Cottages** ⓘ *T0845-268 0785, www.english-country-cottages.co.uk.*

Campsites
Campsites vary greatly in quality and level of facilities. Some sites are only open from April to October. See the following sites: www.pitchup.com; www.coolcamping.com, good for finding characterful sites that allow campfires; www.ukcampsite.co.uk, which is the most comprehensive service with thousands of sites, many with pictures and reviews from punters; and www.campingandcaravanningclub.co.uk. The Forestry Commission have campsites on their wooded estates, see www.campingintheforest.com.

Food and drink in England

Food

Only 30 years ago few would have thought to come to England for haute cuisine. Since the 1980s, though, the English have been determinedly shrugging off their reputation for over-boiled cabbage and watery beef. Now cookery shows like Masterchef are the most popular on TV after the soaps, and thanks in part to the wave of celebrity chefs they have created, you can expect a generally high standard of competence in restaurant kitchens. Towns like Ludlow, Padstow and Whitstable have carved reputations for themselves almost solely on the strength of their cuisine.

Pub food has also been transformed in recent years, and now many of them offer ambitious lunchtime and supper menus in so-called gastro pubs. Most parts of the country still boast regional specialities, including local cheese such as Wensleydale from the Yorkshire Dales. Other specialities in Yorkshire are spankingly fresh seafood, especially from Whitby, as well as fish from the sea and from the farm.

The biggest problem with eating out is the ludicrously limited serving hours in some pubs and hotels, particularly in remoter locations. These places only serve food during restricted hours, generally about 1200-1430 for lunch and 1830-2130 for supper, seemingly ignorant of the eating habits of foreign visitors, or those who would prefer a bit more flexibility during their holiday. In small places especially, it can be difficult finding food outside these enforced times. Places that serve food all day till 2100 or later are restaurants, fast-food outlets and the many chic bistros and café-bars, which can be found not only in the main cities but increasingly in smaller towns. The latter often offer very good value and above-average quality fare.

Drink

Drinking is a national hobby and sometimes a dangerous one at that. **Real ale** – flat, brown beer known as bitter, made with hops – is the national drink, but now struggles to maintain its market share in the face of fierce competition from continental lagers and alcopops. Many small independent breweries are still up and running though, as well as microbreweries attached to individual pubs, which produce far superior ales. **Cider** (fermented apple juice) is also experiencing a resurgence of interest and is a speciality of Somerset. English **wine** is also proving surprisingly resilient: generally it compares favourably with German varieties and many vineyards now offer continental-style sampling sessions.

In many pubs the basic ales are chilled under gas pressure like lagers, but the best ales, such as those from independent breweries, are 'real ales', still fermenting in the cask and served cool but not chilled (around 12°C) under natural pressure from a handpump, electric pump or air pressure fount. There is no shortage of real ale pubs in Yorkshire, home of Tetleys and Theakstons, along with many other microbreweries.

The **pub** is still the traditional place to enjoy a drink: the best are usually freehouses (not tied to a brewery) and feature real log or coal fires in winter, flower-filled gardens for the summer (even in cities occasionally) and most importantly, thriving local custom. Many also offer characterful accommodation and restaurants serving high-quality fare. Pubs are prey to the same market forces as any other business, though, and many a delightful local has recently succumbed to exorbitant property prices or to the bland makeover favoured by the large chains. In 2012, pubs were closing at the rate of 12 a week due to the recession.

Essentials A-Z

Accident and emergency

For police, fire brigade, ambulance and, in certain areas, mountain rescue or coastguard, T999 or T112.

Disabled travellers

Wheelchair users, and blind or partially sighted people are automatically given 34-50% discount on train fares, and those with other disabilities are eligible for the Disabled Person's Railcard, which costs £20 per year and gives a third off most tickets. If you will need assistance at a railway station, call the train company that manages the station you're starting your journey from 24 hours in advance. **Disabled UK** residents can apply to their local councils for a concessionary bus pass. National Express have a helpline for disabled passengers, T08717-818179, to plan journeys and arrange assistance. They also sell a discount coach card for £10 for people with disabilities.

The **English Tourist Board** website, www.visitengland.com, has information on the National Accessible Scheme (NAS) logos to help disabled travellers find the right accommodation for their needs, as well as details of walks that are possible with wheelchairs and the Shopmobility scheme. Many local tourist offices offer accessibility details for their area.

Useful organizations include:
Radar, T020-7250 3222, www.radar.org.uk. A good source of advice and information. It produces an annual National Key Scheme Guide and key for gaining access to over 9000 toilet facilities across the UK.
Tourism for all, T0845-124 9971, www.holidaycare.org.uk, www.tourismfor all.org.uk. An excellent source of information about travel and for identifying accessible accommodation in the UK.

Electricity

The current in Britain is 240V AC. Plugs have 3 square pins and adapters are widely available.

Health

For minor accidents go to the nearest casualty department or an Accident and Emergency (A&E) Unit at a hospital. For other enquiries phone NHS Direct 24 hours (T0845-4647) or visit an NHS walk-in centre. See also individual town and city directories throughout the book for details of local medical services.

Money → *For up-to-date exhange rates, see www.xe.com.*

The British currency is the pound sterling (£), divided into 100 pence (p). Coins come in denominations of 1p, 2p, 5p, 10p, 20p, 50p, £1 and £2. Banknotes come in denominations of £5, £10, £20 and £50. The last of these is not widely used and may be difficult to change.

Banks and bureaux de change

Banks tend to offer similar exchange rates and are usually the best places to change money and cheques. Outside banking hours you'll have to use a bureau de change, which can be easily found at the airports and train stations and in larger cities. **Thomas Cook** and other major travel agents also operate bureaux de change with reasonable rates. Avoid changing money or cheques in hotels, as the rates are usually poor. Main post offices and branches of **Marks and Spencer** will change cash without charging commission.

Credit cards and ATMs

Most hotels, shops and restaurants accept the major credit cards though some places may charge for using them. Some smaller establishments such as B&Bs may only accept cash.

Currency cards

If you don't want to carry lots of cash, prepaid currency cards allow you to preload money from your bank account, fixed at the day's exchange rate. They look like a credit card or debit card and are issued by specialist money changing companies, such as Travelex and Caxton FX. You can top up and check your balance by phone, online and sometimes by text.

Money transfers

If you need money urgently, the quickest way to have it sent to you is to have it wired to the nearest bank via **Western Union**, T0800-833833, www.westernunion.co.uk, or **MoneyGram**, www.moneygram.com. The Post Office can also arrange a MoneyGram transfer. Charges are on a sliding scale; so it will cost proportionately less to wire out more money. Money can also be wired by **Thomas Cook**, www.thomasexchangeglobal.co.uk, or transferred via a bank draft, but this can take up to a week.

Taxes

Most goods are subject to a Value Added Tax (VAT) of 20%, with the major exception of food and books. VAT is usually already included in the advertised price of goods. Visitors from non-EU countries can save money through shopping at places that offer Tax Free Shopping (also known as the Retail Export Scheme), which allows a refund of VAT on goods that will be taken out of the country. Note that not all shops participate in the scheme and that VAT cannot be reclaimed on hotel bills or other services.

Cost of travelling

England can be an expensive place to visit, and London and the south in particular can eat heavily into your budget. There is budget accommodation available, however, and backpackers will be able to keep their costs down. Fuel is a major expense and won't just cost an arm and a leg but also the limbs of all remaining family members, and public transport – particularly rail travel if not booked in advance – can also be pricey, especially for families. Accommodation and restaurant prices also tend to be higher in more popular destinations and during the busy summer months.

The minimum daily budget required, if you're staying in hostels or camping, cycling or hitching (not recommended), and cooking your own meals, will be around £30 per person per day. If you start using public transport and eating out occasionally that will rise to around £35-40. Those staying in slightly more upmarket B&Bs or guesthouses, eating out every evening at pubs or modest restaurants and visiting tourist attractions can expect to pay around £60 per day. If you also want to hire a car and eat well, then costs will rise considerably to at least £75-80 per person per day. Single travellers will have to pay more than half the cost of a double room, and should budget on spending around 60-70% of what a couple would spend.

Opening hours

Businesses are usually open Mon-Sat 0900-1700. In towns and cities, as well as villages in holiday areas, many shops open on a Sun but they will open later and close earlier. For banks, see above. For TIC opening hours, see the tourist information sections in the relevant cities, towns and villages in the text.

Post

Most post offices are open Mon-Fri 0900 to 1730 and Sat 0900-1230 or 1300. Smaller sub-post offices are closed for an hour at lunch (1300-1400) and many of them operate out of a shop. Stamps can be bought at post offices, but also from many shops. A 1st-class letter weighing up to 100 g to anywhere in the UK costs 60p (a large letter over 240 mm by 165 mm is 90p) and should arrive the following day, while 2nd-class letters weighing up to 100 g cost 50p (69p) and take between 2-4 days. For more information about Royal Mail postal services, call T08457-740740, or visit www.royalmail.com.

Safety

Generally speaking, England is a safe place to visit. English cities have their fair share of crime, but much of it is drug-related and confined to the more deprived peripheral areas. Trust your instincts, and if in doubt, take a taxi.

Telephone → *Country code +44.*

Useful numbers: operator T100; international operator T155; directory enquiries T192; overseas directory enquiries T153. Most public payphones are operated by British Telecom (**BT**) and can be found in towns and cities, though less so in rural areas. Numbers of public phone booths have declined in recent years due to the advent of the mobile phone, so don't rely on being able to find a payphone wherever you go. Calls from BT payphones cost a minimum of 60p, for which you get 30 mins for a local or national call. Calls to non-geographic numbers (eg 0845), mobile phones and others may cost more. Payphones take either coins (10p, 20p, 50p and £1), 50c, 1 or 2 euro coins, credit cards or BT Chargecards, which are available at newsagents and post offices displaying the BT logo. These cards come in denominations of £2, £3, £5 and £10. Some payphones also have facilities for internet, text messaging and emailing.

For most countries (including Europe, USA and Canada) calls are cheapest Mon-Fri between 1800 and 0800 and all day Sat-Sun. For Australia and New Zealand it's cheapest to call from 1430-1930 and from 2400-0700 every day. However, the cheapest ways to call abroad from England is not via a standard UK landline provider. Calls are free using **Skype** on the internet, or you can route calls from your phone through the internet with **JaJah** (www.jajah.com) or from a mobile using **Rebtel**. Many phone companies offer discounted call rates by calling their access number prior to dialling the number you want, including www.dialabroad.co.uk and www.simply-call.com.

Area codes are not needed if calling from within the same area. Any number prefixed by 0800 or 0500 is free to the caller; 08457 numbers are charged at local rates and 08705 numbers at the national rate.

Time

Greenwich Mean Time (GMT) is used from late Oct to late Mar, after which time the clocks go forward 1 hr to British Summer Time (BST).

Tipping

Tipping in England is at the customer's discretion. In a restaurant you should leave a tip of 10-15% if you are satisfied with the service. If the bill already includes a service charge, which is likely if you are in a large group, you needn't add a further tip. Tipping is not normal in pubs or bars. Taxi drivers may expect a tip for longer journeys, usually around 10%.

Tourist information

Tourist information centres (TICs) can be found in most towns. Their addresses, phone numbers and opening hours are listed in the relevant sections of this book. Opening hours vary depending on the time of year, and many of the smaller offices are closed or have limited opening hours during the winter months. All tourist offices provide information on accommodation, public transport, local attractions and restaurants, as well as selling books, local guides, maps and souvenirs. Many also have free street plans and leaflets describing local walks. They can also book accommodation for a small fee.

Museums, galleries and historic houses

Over 300 stately homes, gardens and countryside areas, are cared for by the **National Trust** ① *T0844-800 1895, www.nationaltrust.org.uk*. If you're going to be visiting several sights during your stay, then it's worth taking annual membership, which costs £53, £25 if you're aged under 26 and £70 for a family, giving free access to all National Trust properties. A similar organization is **English Heritage** ① *T0870-333 1181, www.english-heritage.org.uk*, which manages hundreds of ancient monuments and other sights around England, including Stonehenge, and focuses on restoration and preservation. Membership includes free admission to sites, and advance information on events, and costs £47 per adult to £82 per couple, under-19s free. **Natural England** ① *T0845-600 3078, www.naturalengland.org.uk*, is concerned with restoring and conserving the English countryside, and can give information on walks and events in the countryside.

Many other historic buildings are owned by local authorities, and admission is cheap, or in many cases free. Most municipal **art galleries** and **museums** are free, as well as most state-owned museums, particularly those in London and other large cities. Most fee-paying attractions give a discount or concession for senior citizens, the unemployed, full-time students and children under 16 (those under five are admitted free in most places). Proof of age or status must be shown.

Finding out more

The best way of finding out more information is to contact Visit England (aka the English Tourist Board), www.visitengland.com. Alternatively, you can contact VisitBritain, the organization responsible for tourism. Both organizations can provide a wealth of free literature and information such as maps, city guides and accommodation brochures. Travellers with special needs should also contact VisitEngland or their nearest VisitBritain office. If you want more detailed information on a particular area, contact the specific tourist boards; see in the main text for details.

Visas and immigration

Visa regulations are subject to change, so it is essential to check with your local British embassy, high commission or consulate before leaving home. Citizens of all European countries – except Albania, Bosnia Herzegovina, Kosovo, Macedonia, Moldova, Turkey, Serbia and all former Soviet republics (other than the Baltic states) – require only a passport to enter Britain and can generally stay for up to 3 months. Citizens of Australia, Canada, New Zealand, South Africa or the USA can stay for up to 6 months, providing they have a return ticket and sufficient funds to cover their stay. Citizens of most other countries require a visa from the commission or consular office in the country of application.

The UK Border Agency, www.ukba.homeoffice.gov.uk, is responsible for UK immigration matters and its website is a good place to start for anyone hoping visit, work, study or emigrate to the UK. For visa extensions also contact the UK Border Agency via the website. Citizens of Australia, Canada, New Zealand, South Africa or the USA wishing to stay longer than 6 months will need an Entry Clearance Certificate from the British High Commission in their country. For more details, contact your nearest British embassy, consulate or high commission, or the Foreign and Commonwealth Office in London.

Weights and measures

Imperial and metric systems are both in use. Distances on roads are measured in miles and yards, drinks poured in pints and gills, but generally, the metric system is used elsewhere.

Contents

Footprint features

York & Central Yorkshire

Picture-perfect and bearing a glossy sheen, the city of York juts out of the rolling hills of the Yorkshire Moors like a real life version of Oz's Emerald City. The awe-inspiring heights of Walter de Grey's cathedral are still so well preserved after hundreds of years that you could be forgiven for wondering if the architect made a deal with the devil that his building should stand forever. But for all its charming antique buildings and winding medieval streets, the countryside around York holds as much allure as the city itself. York sits at the base of the moors, where so many shades of green are to be found that you'll run out of words to describe them. The sprawling North Yorkshire Moors National Park was made to wander in, and so it is traced with walking paths that offer views to take your breath away. Tucked away amidst all that beauty are Helmsley's Norman castle, the ancient abbeys at Rievaulx and Rosedale, and Castle Howard's spectacular monument to foolish wealth. All are an easy drive from York.

Visiting York and Central Yorkshire

Getting there and around York is a major enough city to be easily accessible by **train** and **bus** from most parts of England (see Arriving in York below). However, while you can easily get to, and around York without a car, getting around the countryside is another issue. Most villages and sights are only infrequently served by **coach**, and not at all by train. ▸▸ *See Transport, page 35.*

Tourist information All of Yorkshire is covered by the Yorkshire Tourist Board ① *www.yorkshire.com*, which has offices in York and Thirsk. Its website features good background information on the region and ideas for walks. Another good walking guide is the AA's *50 Walks in North Yorkshire*.

York

Coveted by emperors, Vikings and kings, and known for centuries as the capital of the North, York's enduring beauty can be attributed largely to the simple fact that it was somehow overlooked by the Industrial Revolution. Its medieval alleyways were never bulldozed and replaced by wide, straight streets. Its Norman castle walls were not torn down to make room for a handy roadway around the centre of town. Its medieval churches were not replaced by Starbucks cafés. So now, centuries after it left the national stage as a political city of any influence, it sits as a sort of memorandum from the past. Its grand edifices and ferociously protective walls seem to state defiantly, 'Once this town was important. Once men died to protect it. Once upon a time...' For this is a once upon a time kind of a place – and it's worth mentioning that modern York lies prostrate before the altar of tourism. Still, overrun though it is by trainloads of day-tripping Londoners cramming into its antique shops, hordes of European schoolchildren ignoring its architecture and coachloads of Americans queuing in front of the too-many too-quaint teashops, York demands to be visited. And there are ample places to hide from the crowds: tiny ancient churches, dark and winding streets that seem to go on for miles and stretches of city wall where you'll be completely alone. ►► *For listings, see pages 32-35.*

Arriving in York

Getting there York is on the east coast mainline, and is served by **Arriva CrossCountry, Grand Central Rail** and **First TransPennine Express.** From London King's Cross, **trains** to York run every 30 minutes; the journey takes approximately 2 hours. Trains arrive at York Station, at the edge of the city walls across the River Ouse about a 15-minute walk from the centre of town. By **car**, York is 20 minutes' drive from the M1/M62 motorway. **Coaches** and regional **buses** pick up and drop off passengers about 200 m north of the train station on Rougier Street, near Lendal Bridge, although many coach services also drop passengers off at the train station itself. ►► *See Transport, page 35.*

Getting around This is a tiny city, best handled on **foot. Taxis** are plentiful when it all gets to be a bit too much, but you can easily walk from one city wall clear across town to the other in about 15 minutes. With all of its pedestrianized sections and its strictly limited parking, driving takes longer and is more difficult than walking. City bus routes are operated by **First,** T01904-551400, www.firstgroup.com. This is such a tourist town that the most common vehicle on the tangled streets of York seems to be the tour bus. There are dozens to choose from, and you can find brochures for most of them in the tourist office if you fancy adding to the road congestion. On the other hand, there are equally as many guided walks about, and these are often more interesting and hands-on. Some of the best, and completely free, are led by the **York Association of Voluntary Guides** ① *T01904-640780, http://avgyork.co.uk,* which generally meet daily at 1015 outside York Art Gallery in Exhibition Square. There is an additional tour at 1315 Friday-Sunday from November to March and at 1415 from April to October.

Tourist information York's tourist offices are the biggest and best in Yorkshire. **Main TIC** ① *1 Museum St, T01904-550099, www.visityork.org, Mon-Sat 0900-1700 (1730 Jul-Aug), Sun 1000-1600.* The website has free PDF guides to download. The TIC sells the York Pass, a card that can be used at over 30 local attractions, available for one to three consecutive days, starting at £34 for one day, under-16s £18. The YAT pass allows unlimited entry for 12 months to the JORVIK Viking Centre, DIG, Barley Hall and Micklegate Bar Museum, £16, under-16s £11.25.

Background

Nobody knows exactly who it was that first chose to settle in the sheltered, marshy area between the rivers Ouse and Foss at the edge of the Yorkshire Moors, but it was the

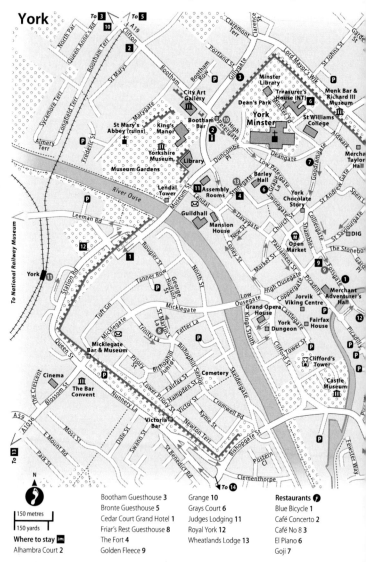

York

To 3   **To 5**

Where to stay 🛏

Alhambra Court **2**
Bootham Guesthouse **3**
Bronte Guesthouse **5**
Cedar Court Grand Hotel **1**
Friar's Rest Guesthouse **8**
The Fort **4**
Golden Fleece **9**
Grange **10**
Grays Court **6**
Judges Lodging **11**
Royal York **12**
Wheatlands Lodge **13**

Restaurants 🍴

Blue Bicycle **1**
Café Concerto **2**
Café No 8 **3**
El Piano **6**
Goji **7**

150 metres
150 yards

Romans who first put York on the map. The site where the city now stands was once a critical part of Roman England. While conquering the north of England, Roman soldiers camped where York is now, and found the site to be so well located for defence purposes

that they built a permanent fort there and named it Eboracum – believed to be a slightly uncreative name meaning 'the place of the yew trees'. A century later, Eboracum was a thriving Roman village, home to 6000 soldiers and the de facto headquarters for all troops in northern England. While very little remains of the structures that housed the troops, extensive Roman artefacts have been discovered that give a clear indication that, as early as AD 180, York was a substantial, bustling city. Streets like Stonegate and Petergate are believed to follow the routes of the Roman streets once known as Via Praetoria and Via Principalis.

Saxon invaders were the next to take over the area, and they, too, valued York, making it the capital of the regional state of Deira. They renamed it Eoforwic, and promptly began adding onto the Roman structures and battlements. In 625, King Edwin of Northumbria married Princess Aethelburga, a Christian. As there were no churches in the area at the time in which to hold the ceremony, the king ordered one built, and a plain, wooden chapel was built on the site of what is now the Minster. Saxons were followed by Vikings, who found the city offered a handy base to use while raping and pillaging the countryside. They modified the Saxon name to sound more familiar, calling it Jorvik. Viking street names remain the same – in fact, as it is in York, the term 'gate' was used to mean 'street' in Viking dialects.

William the Conquerer also made York his military headquarters. Normans rebuilt the city in stone, using the old Viking structures as a foundation for their architecture. This medieval period of construction is responsible for much of the city's appearance today, and most of its

Il Paradiso del Cibo 4
Melton's Too 12
Pig & Pastry 14

Pubs & bars 🍸
Ackhorne 8

Black Swan 5
Blue Bell 9
Lamb & Lion 10
York Tap 11
Yorkshire Terrier Inn 13

religious structures. Work began on the current Minster in 1220, and continued for more than 200 years. Dozens of churches and abbeys were built in the city during this time, and many of them survive today

As the inescapable tour guides tell their charges at the beginning of virtually every foray through town: in York the streets are called gates, the gates are called bars and the bars are called pubs. Sure it's silly, but once you've got that down, it all makes a little more sense. The most significant sights in York are all contained within its rambling city walls, but the streets wind and wander in a quaint but confusing fashion that all but guarantees that you'll spend some of your time here lost. But that's fine, really, as that might be the moment when you stumble across a beautiful piece of history all your own.

Bootham Bar

A good place to start any walk through town is at Bootham Bar, the oldest of the four city gateways, dating, in part, from the 11th century, although most of it was built over the subsequent two centuries. It offers entrance to the city via High Petergate. This is the only of the four gates that sits on the site of one of the original entrances to the old Roman fortress. It bears the Stuart coat of arms, and still has its original wooden portcullis.

Across the busy intersection from the gate is **Exhibition Square**, with its unimpressive fountain and a chunk of the old walls. This is where you'll find the **York Art Gallery** ① *Exhibition Sq, T01904-687687, www.yorkartgallery.org*, which is closed until Easter 2015 for major revelopment.

Next to the gallery is the **King's Manor**, which once formed part of the abbot's lodging of **St Mary's Abbey**, which lies in ruins not far away. Sections of the manor date from 1270, although most of it is was built in the late 1400s. After the Dissolution it was taken over by the Lord President of the Council of the North, after which it was used as a royal headquarters in Yorkshire. During its time the manor was visited by James I, Charles I and Henry VIII. It's now used by the University of York.

Museum Gardens

Just a short distance down St Leonard's Place from the Manor, past the endless queues waiting for tour buses, is the lovely green space of the Museum Gardens, where a cluster of ruins sit in various stages of decay. To the right of the entrance are the remains of **St Leonard's Hospital**, which was founded in the 12th century. Nearby stands the **Multangular Tower**, which has a fourth-century Roman base and a medieval top; inside is a collection of Roman coffins unearthed in and around York. The gardens lead up to the **Yorkshire Museum** ① *T01904-687687, www.yorkshiremuseum.orq.uk, daily 1000-1700, £7.50, under-16s free, with York Minster £12, under-16s free*, with its extensive display of artefacts collected in the region. Included in the collection are pieces of the old Roman gateway to the city, Viking artefacts and the Middleham Jewel, believed to be one of the finest examples of medieval jewellery found in Britain. The museum's basement includes the original fireplace and walls of **St Mary's Abbey**, which was founded in 1080. The rest of the craggy abbey ruins are nearby, but there's not much left of them – just a few sections of the old walls and a row of apses. In the Museum Gardens is the **York Observatory** ① *Thu and Sat 1130-1430, free*, the oldest working one of its kind in the county.

Spooksville

"We have travelled extensively working on research projects across the globe and nowhere have we found more ghosts than in historic York." So said Jason Karl, president of the Ghost Research Foundation International, when, in 2002, he named York the most haunted city in Europe. The city was so proud of this award that it promptly put out a press release, which only slightly had a 'See? We told you we had ghosts' ring about it. In fact, reports of apparitions scaring the bejesus out of living folk go back hundreds of years here. Not just ghosts but *battalions* of spooks. A plumber's apprentice working in the Treasurer's House in 1953 reported seeing an entire Roman legion, led by a centurion on horseback, marching through the basement. His detailed description of their uniforms was first used to discredit him – such uniforms had never been heard of by archaeologists – and then to back him up, when descriptions of uniforms matching those he'd seen were actually found. King's Manor is haunted by a monk, thought to be from the adjacent St Mary's Abbey, and by a lady in a green Tudor

dress, who holds a bouquet of roses. Patrons in the Old Starre Inn, on Stonegate, have heard the groans of Cavaliers, whose wounded were brought to the stables behind the inn during the Civil War. There's also an old woman ghost who climbs the stairs there, and two spectral black cats. A decapitated Thomas Percy is said to wander blindly around the Church of Holy Trinity on Goodramgate in search of his head. He was executed in 1572 for treason against Elizabeth I, and he's unlikely to find his head as it was impaled on a pike above Mickelgate Bar. If you choose to stay at The Snickleway Inn on Goodramgate, you might encounter a whole houseful of ghosts. Among them is one which has never actually been seen, but which wafts by, leaving the scent of lavender in its path (lavender was used to hide the stench of death during plagues). There's also a ghost of a Victorian child who sits on the stairs. If you're not the jumpy type, there's something vaguely satisfying about York being haunted. It would seem a shame to waste such a historically preserved town on living people like us.

Entering the city walls through **Bootham Bar** offers the option of heading into the town centre or of taking a wander down the old walls. The quarter-mile of castle wall between Bootham and **Monk Bar** is particularly well preserved and offers excellent views of the city and its cathedral. The watchtowers along the wall have been converted to resting points with benches, although in the summertime you'll never be allowed to rest for a second between tour groups clambering up for the view. The imposing and gloomy Monk Bar dates from the 14th century, and is the tallest of the city's old gates. All four gates have their original portcullises, but Monk Bar is the only one in full working order. Inside it is the particularly cheesy **Richard III Museum** ① *T01904-634191, www.richardiiimuseum.co.uk, daily Mar-Oct 0900-1700, mid-Jul to mid-Sep until 2000, Nov-Feb 0930-1600, £3, under-16s free*, one of several pseudo-museums in town with virtually no artefacts. The gate is a magnificent building, though, with tiny cells and precarious stairways between the levels that give an excellent indication of what it must have been like for those who lived and worked here 600 years ago. There is also an exhibition of Richard III's trial and an execution chamber.

The Minster

① T0844-939 0011, www.yorkminster.org. Mon-Sat 0900-1700, Sun 1200-1700, except when it's open for services only; see the What's on section of the website for details. Minster and tower £14, under-16s £3.50, including guided tour and entry to the Orb; minster only £9/free, tower only £5/free.

If you walk into town through Bootham Bar down High Petergate, you're essentially following in Roman footsteps on a route they called Via Principalis. The street curves a short distance past restaurants, pubs and shops and leads directly to where the extraordinary **York Minster** soars above low-slung York. The single most important historic building in all of Yorkshire, and the largest medieval cathedral in Britain, its pale towers are over 60 m tall and can be seen from miles away. Not bad for a church that was started as little more than a quickly built place in which to baptise a king. Its name is actually a misnomer: it is called a 'minster', which comes from the Latin *monasterium*, but it never served as a monastery. It stands on the site of the old Roman military headquarters, and impressive remains from Roman and Norman times have been found in its foundations. One of the most significant of the Roman finds stands to the right of the Minster in the form of the incongruously simple Roman column, which was unearthed in the Minster's basement and re-erected nearby in 1971, on the city's 1900th birthday. Historians believe the column was part of a huge Roman hall (the *Principia*) that once stood where the Minster is now.

More recently, as part of a five-year restoration project due to be completed in 2016, excavation on the Minster's basement has revealed a wealth of archaeological finds. Archaeologists discovered evidence of an Anglo-Saxon settlement, complete with its own mint, and Viking human remains. These findings and more will be detailed in new interactive galleries in the Undercroft (see below), due to open in summer 2013.

A church has stood on this site for 1300 years. The earliest known church on this plot of soil was a wooden structure built in 627 for the baptism of King Edwin of Northumbria. It was later replaced in stone, but that building was destroyed in William the Conqueror's 'Harrying of the North'. The Norman archbishop Thomas of Bayeux oversaw the reconstruction that began in 1080, and the remains of that building can still be seen in the foundation and the crypt. The current Minster was begun in 1220, when Archbishop Walter de Grey ordered a church built to rival Canterbury's cathedral. Construction took 250 years, which explains why the building contains so many architectural styles – over and over again, the construction process outlived the designers. The south transept was the first section completed in 1240, and the north transept the second in 1260. By the time the nave was completed in 1345, de Grey was long dead. The choir was completed in 1405 and the towers in 1480, bringing construction, at last, to an end.

The crowning glory of York Minster is its glass. The most beautiful example is the heart-shaped **West Window,** which was created in 1338. The oldest glass is to be found in the second bay window in the northern aisle of the nave. Created in 1155, it contains the oldest stained glass in the country. While in the nave, take note of the ceiling which, while made of wood (it was built in 1840 to replace the previous roof destroyed by fire), has been painted to resemble stone. Throughout the rest of the Minster, the roof is actual stone.

At the cathedral's crossing is the north transept's **Five Sisters Window,** which gets its name from its five thin 15-m tall panes. Near the window a vestibule leads to the **Chapter House.** Built in the 13th century, it contains some of the finest decorated stonework in the country. Unusually, the vaulted wooden roof of the octagonal Chapter House stands without the support of a central column.

Back in the Cathedral, the window directly opposite the Five Sisters is the elaborate **Rose Window**, which was built to mark the marriage of Henry VII and Elizabeth of York in 1486. Also in the crossing is de Grey's own austere tomb.

In the centre of the crossing, the **Choir** is separated from the **Nave** by a fascinating stone rood screen. Dating to the late 15th century, it features life-size statues of all the English kings (up to that date) except for Henry VI. At the end of the east aisle is the most impressive window in the Minster: the remarkable and awe-inspiring **East Window**, which, at 24 m by 10 m, is recognized as the world's largest medieval stained-glass window. Created around 1405 by John Thornton, its themes are varied, and include the beginning and the end of the world, with the upper panels telling the story of the Old Testament, and the lower panels the grim predictions of Revelations. Unfortunately, if understandably, visitors are kept so far from the window that, without binoculars, it's virtually impossible to make those scenes out. It's all a lovely, massive blur. They actually show strange interpretations of the Bible, with scenes of Adam and Eve being handed apples by a creature that is half-snake/half-woman and inexplicably winged. Another shows a drunken Noah being glared at by his family, while a third shows his ark populated by a handful of people and a whippet. Now, though, there is a new gallery called the Orb in a futuristic metallic dome which allows visitors to get a closer look at the stained glass panels in the East Window. Next to the Orb, in St Stephen's Chapel and All Saints Chapel, are some interactive displays detailing the conservation work happening on the East Window, such as stone masonry.

In the south transept are stairs down to the foundations or **undercroft**, which has been converted into one of the most fascinating museums in all of Yorkshire. The space under the church was excavated in the 1960s during restoration work. While the work was underway, archaeologists uncovered extensive Roman and Norman relics that have been preserved here. Also found were the original foundations of the Roman fort, as well as extensive sculpture and stonework from the original Norman church. All are well displayed and arranged. Some sections – with Norman tombs for babies – are quite moving. From the undercroft you can visit the treasury, with silver plate pilfered from de Grey's tomb, and the cold and gloomy crypt, which contains interesting remnants of the 1080 church. A small doorway in the crypt opens onto the base of a pillar that was once part of the guardhouse of the original Roman camp.

Finally, before leaving the church, if you're not afraid of heights you can climb to the top of the **central tower** for unbeatable bird's eye views of the city.

Around the Minster

The large green park through an arched gateway directly beside the Minster is **Dean's Park**, which makes a pleasant space for a picnic on sunny afternoons. The arched architectural fragments along its far edge are part of a Norman archbishop's palace, and if you follow the path that cuts through the park you'll reach the 13th-century chapel that holds the **York Minster Library** ① *Mon-Fri 0900-1700*. It's here that you'll find the baptismal records for one of York's most famous sons, Guy Fawkes. Continuing through the park (and following the signs) is the **Treasurer's House** ① *T01904-624247, www.nationaltrust.org, Sat-Thu 1100-1630, £5.90, under-16s £2.95*, just outside the

Minster grounds. The 17th-century building looks startlingly modern compared to its more ancient neighbours, but it's excellently preserved and has lovely gardens. It is most popular with fans of period furnishings, as it is outfitted appropriately to its age, and there are regular tours of the interior, including ones in the basement about ghosts of Roman soldiers. For those for whom a chair is a chair, the gardens out front are free.

On the other side of the Minster from Dean's Park is one of the oldest buildings in York. **St William's College** ① *open for private hire only*, is a half-timbered building that dates to 1467. Its name refers back to when it served as a school for the Minster's chantry priests. At other times it has been the Royal Mint and the king's printers.

Stonegate

The streets around the Minster are sprawling shopping lanes, filled with tourist boutiques, tourist restaurants and tourist pubs. The most impressive of these streets is Stonegate, surely the most photographed street in all of York. This medieval lane made of the same stone as the Minster traces its history back to Roman times when it was called Via Praetoria. Today it is lined with antique jewellery shops and boutiques selling sweaters made of Yorkshire wool. Day and night it is packed with tourists, not least because it makes a handy cut-through from the Minster area down to Lendal Street along the river. Despite the constant throngs, it is still charming in its medieval completeness. This is also the street where Guy Fawkes' parents lived (look for the plaque). Sneaking down the little medieval pedestrian alleys – called (delightfully) snickleways or ginnels – that lead off can be rewarding. One ginnel leads to a rare fragment of a Norman house, while others lead to pubs and teashops. Look for the little red devil that squats on the wall outside No 33. Little figures like this one, high on the walls, once served as adverts or signs for the shops underneath them. This is one of the most unusual in York, and is believed to have served as a sign for a printworks once located here; printer's assistants were once called 'printers' devils'. Another intriguing figure can be seen at the head of Stonegate, at the intersection of High Petergate, where Minerva lounges on a stack of books up by the street signs. She marks the site of where a 19th-century bookseller operated out of a corner shop. The snickleway beside the red devil is known as **Coffee Yard**, and, at 70 m, is one of the longest in York. It's also one of the most used cut-throughs by locals, as it connects Stonegate with Grape Lane, with its pleasant restaurants, cafés and quality shops.

Lendal Street

If you're not carried away by the lure of ginnels, from Stonegate you can wander down to Lendal Street toward **St Helen's Square** where there is usually a hubbub with local street musicians entertaining the crowds. This is where you'll find the famed **Bettys** tearoom where it's been since 1945. People queue for hours through much of the day for a pricey cuppa here, but it's worth noting that before 1030 you can usually waltz right in for a breakfast scone. At one corner of the square, kind of tucked away, is the small but lovely 13th-century **St Helen's church**. The front of the church is sort of a trip through the ages, as the base is 13th-century, the capital 15th-century and the bowl 12th-century. Lendal turns into a wide shopping lane from here, with all the usual high street names, so unless you're in the market for some clothes, head back into the medieval town centre where Low Petergate leads to Goodramgate.

The Shambles

If you aren't lost by the time you stumble onto the Shambles, just at the edge of King's Square at the southern end of Goodramgate, you will be shortly. The narrow, crowded shopping lanes that run off this street are generally overrated in terms of the shops they hold, but absolutely unmatchable in sheer historic charm. So old is this section of town, that it is the only street in York mentioned by name in the *Domesday Book* of 1086, which also lists the half-brother of William the Conquerer as owning a stall on the Shambles. While most of the stores today are the sadly predictable hocus-pocus magick shoppes or tepid stationery stores or sellers of Scottish/Irish/Yorkshire woollens, the streets are lined with wonderfully photogenic ancient timber-framed buildings. Once the city's butchers' quarter, it's easy to imagine what it must have been like to come here for a bit of meat for dinner when it was a teeming, stinking pit. The sharp-eyed will notice that some buildings still have old meat hooks hanging from their exterior walls. The similarly overrated, but no less charming **Newgate Market** is at one end of the Shambles as well, but you're unlikely to find anything to take home from it aside from a snapshot. Near the Shambles is York's most whimsically named street – **Whip-ma-Whap-ma-Gate**. Don't believe any explanations given to you by locals as to the derivation of the name; the sad truth is, nobody remembers anymore. It is one of history's curiosities.

At the top of the Shambles is **York's Chocolate Story** ① *King's Sq, T0845-498 9411, www.yorkchocolatestory.com, daily 1000-1800, entry by 1-hr tour only, every 10-20 mins, £9.50 (£8.50 online), under-16s £7.50 (£6),* which opened in 2012 to mixed reviews. As home to Joseph Rowntree and Terry's, producers of such iconic confectionery as Kitkat and Terry's Chocolate Orange, it's not surprising that York has its very own chocolate museum, albeit a small one. There are interactive exhibits and a chocolatier stages a demonstration.

Around the castle

The Shambles are a short stroll from the castle section of town, such as it is. This is the more modern section of York, with shopping centres and vast car parks. **Coppergate**, once the busiest street in Viking York, is no less crowded now that it is an über-high street. It tries to part you from your money over and over again throughout its length. Buskers sing sad songs outside unattractive buildings, and it's all more than a little depressing. At the end of the street is the much-hyped **Jorvik Viking Centre** ① *T01904-615505, jorvik-viking-centre.co.uk, daily Apr-Oct 1000-1700 (last admission), Oct half term until 1800, Nov-Mar 0900-1600, £9.75, under-16s £9.75, free with a YAT pass, see page 19, it's worth booking in advance during busy school holidays.* Now, the people of York are so damn proud of this place that it seems churlish not to marvel at it. The main part is largely a recreation of a Viking village, where you sit in a 'time capsule' as you're motored smoothly past plastic blacksmiths and marketers of the Viking era. The selling point is the fact that the faces of the 'people' in the museum were based on Viking skulls found in the area, so this is probably what the early inhabitants did look like, and there are authentic smells and sounds as well. There's also a reconstruction of the original archaeological site and an interactive museum.

Nearby on Castlegate is the Georgian **Fairfax House** ① *T01904-655543, www.fairfaxhouse.co.uk, Tue-Sat and bank holiday Mon 1000-1700, Sun 1230-1600, entrance by 1-hr guided tour only at 1100 and 1400, no advance booking required, closed Jan* *and early Feb, £6, under-16s free,* another one of those lovely historic houses restored with period furnishings. This one has the added attraction of containing the 18th-century art collection of chocolate magnate Noel Terry. It provides a remarkably vivid snapshot of upper-class domestic life in Georgian times.

Not far from the Viking centre on Fossgate is the **Merchant Adventurers' Hall** ① *T01904-654818, www.theyorkcompany.co.uk, Mar-Oct Mon-Thu 0900-1700, Fri-Sat 0900-1530, Sun 1100-1400, Nov-Feb 1000-1600, Fri-Sat 1000-1530, £6, under-16s free,* a gorgeous timber-framed hall once owned by the region's leading businessmen and wool traders. Its sheer beauty and historic completion are the primary reasons for sticking your head round the door, and it also has some interesting furniture and paintings.

On nearby St Saviourgate is **DIG** ① *St Saviour's Church, T01904-615505, digyork.com, daily 1000-1700, entry by tour only, book in advance during busy periods, £5.50, under-16s £5, DIG and JORVIK £13.25, under-16s £10, free entry with the YAT pass, see page 19,* a museum under the same ownership as the JORVIK Viking Museum, giving a hands-on experience of being an archaeologist. Aimed more at children than adults, tours are led by archaeologists who show how to unearth artefacts in copies of excavation pits with Roman, Vikings, Medieval and Victorian remains.

As for the **Castle** itself, aside from the city walls, all that's left is the sparse keep called **Clifford's Tower** ① *T01904-646940, www.english-heritage.org.uk, daily 1000-1600, £4, under-16s £2.40,* which despite standing ignobly on its mound in the centre of a modern car park has a fascinating and dark history. This version was built in the mid-1200s. The old Norman keep was destroyed quite infamously in 1109 during a pogrom in which 150 Jews were hidden there to protect them from an anti-Semitic mob, which then surrounded the building and waited to kill them. Forced to choose between starvation and murder, the Jews committed mass suicide by setting their own prison aflame. It's got an interesting model of what the castle looked like and there are some superb panoramic views of York.

Around the corner from Clifford's Tower the **York Dungeon** ① *12 Clifford St, T0871-423 2260, www.thedungeons.com, daily Apr-Oct 1000-1630, until 1730 Aug, Easter and Whitsun, Nov-Dec 1100-1600, entry by 70-min tour only, £15.60 (online £11), under-16s £11.40 (£8), no children under 10 allowed,* is due to reopen at the time of writing. It promises to be better than ever, with live renactments of events in York's past using real actors portraying the city's famous historic characters, including Guy Fawkes and Dick Turpin.

Across the car park is the wonderfully eccentric **Castle Museum** ① *T01904-687687, www.yorkcastlemuseum.org.uk, daily 0930-1700, £8.50, under-16s free, some galleries will be closed in 2013 due to installation of a major new exhibit opening in Easter 2014,* with its bizarre and extensive collection of artefacts through the ages. These were amassed by one mysterious man, a Dr Kirk from nearby Pickering, who decided 80 years ago that somebody should protect the pieces of the area's heritage or all would be lost. So he gathered everything he could, including pieces belonging to his patients who handed them over instead of cash for treatment. The museum is actually located in an old debtors' prison, and includes a little bit of everything, from the ancient to the very recent. His recreation of a medieval York street is quite magnificent, and some of the pieces he found – including a Viking helmet found in excavations on Coppergate – are truly impressive. Outside is a recently restored Victorian watermill, which operates most weekends 1100-1300.

Elsewhere in York

One of the least visited of the city's bars is **Walmgate Bar** (which is located far from the action at the end of Fossgate), and more's the pity as it is the only gate in the country to retain its barbican. The 14th-century walls still bear the scars from the Civil War battles that took place here in 1644. Once the most important of the four, as it oversaw the main road to York from London, and once serving as a prison for the wealthy, the last gate, **Micklegate Bar** ① *T01904-615505, micklegatebar.com, daily mid-Feb to Mar and Nov 1000-1600, Apr-Oct 1000-1600, closed Dec-Jan and if the city walls are not open, £3.50, Under-16s £2, free with a YAT pass, see page 19*, today holds another one of those pointless museums-without-artefacts, designed more to amuse than to educate. There's a fun dressing up area for children, including some helmets to try on, and a few interesting displays on the War of the Roses and the Battle of Towton, but not much else.

Past Micklegate Bar and the York train station is one of the best museums in the country. The **National Railway Museum** ① *Leeman Rd, T0844-815 3139, www.nrm.org.uk, daily 1000-1800, free*, is a vast, exhaustive, extraordinary facility detailing the history and engineering of train travel in Britain. The enormous museum contains more than 50 locomotives dating back to the early 1800s, all still in working order, along with gorgeously restored railcars that date back to the 1700s, some splendid and rich, others definitely second class. There's memorabilia galore, with posters, charts, adverts and bits and pieces of train history sure to have trainspotters refusing ever to leave.

Around York

Within an hour's drive of York the countryside changes, as the flat farmland gives way to the rolling hills of the moors. Between the city and the hills are a series of charming villages, with their ancient edifices and grand buildings reminders of past wealth.

Castle Howard

① *T01653-648333, www.castlehoward.co.uk, Easter-Oct and late Nov to mid-Dec, house 1100-1600 (last admission), grounds and adventure playground 1000-1730 (last admission 1630); Jan-Easter and first 3 weeks of Nov, grounds and adventure playground only 1000-1600 (last admission 1530). House and grounds £14, concessions £12, under 16s £7.50; grounds only, £9.50, concessions £9, under-16s £6. Well signposted off the A64 towards Scarborough, 15 miles northeast of York.*

In 1772, Horace Walpole wrote of Castle Howard: 'Nobody ... had informed me that I should at one view see a palace, a town, a fortified city, temples on high places, woods worthy of being each a metropolis of the Druids, vales connected to hills by other woods, the noblest lawn in the world fenced by half the horizon, and a mausoleum that would tempt one to be buried alive; in short I have seen gigantic places before, but never a sublime one.' While that might be overstating it a little, it is *only* a little. This fantastic building among the farmland about 15 miles north of York has an irresistible lure to anybody who followed breathlessly the trials and tribulations of the upper classes in the TV series *Brideshead Revisited*. The extraordinary manor house that served as a backdrop to that 1970s programme was Castle Howard. With its domed roof and Grecian-style statues, this vast building stands as proof that some people have more money than sense. Not a castle at all, but a mansion with ambition, the Baroque building was designed in

1699 by Sir John Vanbrugh and Nicholas Hawksmoor for Charles Howard, the third Earl of Carlisle. Vanbrugh, who was not an architect, designed and oversaw the construction of the main house until its completion in 1712, and was working on the rest of the building when he died in 1726. Vanbrugh's lack of construction and design experience has led many experts to speculate that Hawksmoor had much influence on the design of the building. Nobody knows precisely what Howard was thinking when he chose Vanbrugh to design his home, although some speculate that he simply liked his fellow nobleman personally. But amateur though he was, Vanbrugh obviously had a knack, as Hawksmoor later agreed to work with him on Blenheim Palace.

The sheer length of time it took to complete the structure affected its design. While the central building is elaborate, with a large dome, rooftop statues, and fussy detail, the house's two wings are in slightly different styles. The west wing, in particular, completed in the late 1700s, is much simpler in style than the main building, reflecting changes in architectural tastes over the course of that century. But the dominance of the central structure means that you barely notice the lack of perfect balance in the wings. The inside of the building is, if anything, even more over the top than the exterior, filled as it is with paintings by Rubens and Van Dyck, along with so many Chippendale chairs sitting below friezes and plasterwork frills that the mind boggles. The word 'gaudy' doesn't just come to mind, it leaps into the cerebellum.

The thousand acres of **grounds** are better, really, than the house. Even before you reach the building you drive through one unnecessary-but-beautiful archway after another. In the front of the house, a huge fountain gushes amidst statuary and perfectly manicured hedges. Peacocks saunter across the grounds and glower at visitors from the shade of trees. Vanbrugh's excess is here again in the form of man-made lakes that glitter in the distance, and the pointlessly lovely **Temple to the Four Winds** that lures you to take the necessary hike to find it. Then there's the family **mausoleum**, which towers impressively. The extensive walled gardens have a way of keeping horticultural types absorbed for hours. When it all becomes too much, as it likely will, you can take a seat in the house's teashop and rest your feet for the duration of a cream tea. If the kids are getting tetchy about all the adult stuff, take them down to the adventure playground by the lake, wander the nature trails or take a boat trip across the lake if the weather's fine. This is the Disneyland of manor houses.

Kirkham Priory

ⓘ *T01653-618768, www.english-heritage.org.uk, Apr-Sep 1000-1800, Oct-Mar Sat-Sun 1000-1600, £3.40, under-16s £2, off the A64, 5 miles southwest of Malton.*
Just a few miles from Castle Howard, the scant remains of this Augustinian priory attracts few visitors, and that's a shame if only because while there's not much left of the building itself, the setting is spectacular. The 14th-century ruins sit in a green valley beside the slow-moving River Derwent. It is one of the most peaceful, naturally gorgeous locations of any of England's old abbeys.

Thirsk

The bustling town of Thirsk, 23 miles north of York, once home to the world's most famous veterinarian, is a trifle disappointing in quite a few ways. James Herriot's village idyll is not the good-sized town, with traffic and impatient drivers, modern buildings

Walks in Yorkshire

- **Haworth Moor:** 11 miles one-way. Start: Haworth. A bracing climb up on to the moors past Wuthering Heights and down through the wooded valley of Hebden Water to Hebden Bridge. OS Maps: Outdoor Leisure 21.
- **Bolton Abbey:** 6 miles there and back. Start: Bolton Abbey, 5 miles east of Skipton. A gentle riverside walk up the Wharfe valley to find the Strid Wood Nature Trail. OS Maps: Outdoor Leisure 2.
- **Leeds and Liverpool Canal:** 4 miles there and back. Start: Gargrave, 4 miles west of Skipton. Another gentle stroll along an attractive stretch of canal from Gargrave to Bank Newton. OS Maps: Outdoor Leisure 2.
- **Stoodley Pike:** 4 miles there and back. Start: Hebden Bridge. A stiff walk up to the monument and viewpoint overlooking the town. OS Maps: Outdoor Leisure 21.
- **Robin Hood's Bay:** 7 miles there and back. Start: Robin Hood's Bay, 5 miles south of Whitby. A coastal fossil-rich clifftop walk south along part of the Cleveland Way to Ravenscar. OS Maps: Outdoor Leisure 27.
- **Wheeldale Moor:** 6 miles there and back. Start: Goathland, 8 miles south west of Whitby. A walk up onto the moors past Mallyan Spout waterfall to find the remains of a Roman road called Wade's Causeway. OS Maps: Outdoor Leisure 27.
- **Rye Dale:** 8 miles there and back. Start: Helmsley. A walk past Duncombe Park and up the lovely Rye Dale towards Rievaulx Abbey. OS Maps: Outdoor Leisure 26.
- **Whernside:** 5 miles there and back. Start: Chapel Le Dale. A well-trodden but enjoyable hike up to the top of the highest peak in Yorkshire Dales, 2419 ft high. OS Maps: Outdoor Leisure 2.
- **Littondale:** 4 miles there and back. Start: Halton Gill. A secluded moorland walk up onto the hill of above one of the Dales' more peaceful valleys. OS Maps: Outdoor Leisure 2.

and high street shops that you see before you. You'll find no stone cottages, sheep or lowing cattle here. There's a hint of the old medieval Thirsk in the large, colourful **market place**, but it all gets lost in the traffic jams. There are a few Georgian homes on and around Kirkgate, near the market.

The moderately interesting **Thirsk Museum** ⓘ *14-16 Kirkgate, T01845-527707, www.thirskmuseum.org, Easter-Oct Mon-Wed Fri-Sat 1000-1600, £2, under-16s free*, does its best to make up for the modern look of the town by telling you what it looked like back when it was charming. But just about everybody who comes here breezes past that museum and heads to the nearby **World of James Herriot museum** ⓘ *23 Kirkgate, T01845-524234, www.worldofjamesheriot.org, daily Mar-Oct 1000-1700, Nov-Feb until 1600, £8.50, under-16s £5*. The vast size of the car parks near this facility give a good idea of what people are here for. Thirsk claims rightful ownership to being the town that Herriott called 'Darrowby' in his books, and it was here that the author, whose real name was Alf Wight, worked as a veterinarian. The museum – inside his animal surgery, Skeldale House – is dedicated to his life and practice. The years of work, and £1.4 million in cash, that went into creating this ode to Alf paid off, though, as the museum is an entertaining and painstaking recreation of living quarters for the 1940s and 50s and sets of the TV series *All Creatures Great and Small*. Along with a peek at how Wight might have lived, there are also displays on veterinary work past and present. Interactive exhibits examine horse dentistry, as well as the strength needed to calve a cow.

York and Central Yorkshire listings

For hotel and restaurant price codes and other
relevant information, see page 9-12.

see page 9-12.

🛏 Where to stay

York *p18, map p20*

York is a tourist town, so hotels abound, and B&Bs even more so. While accommodation is scattered about, Bootham and Clifton streets have the highest concentration, and are particularly good places to go hunting for a room if you've arrived without reservations. The tourist office in the train station will also book a room for you. However, be prepared for high prices, even for a modest B&B.

££££-£££ Grays Court, Chapter House St, T01904-612613, grayscourt.com. Near the Minster, this small but perfectly formed hotel shares a historic building with a tearoom (the **Parlour**) and art gallery. Some sections date from the 11th century and there is plenty of original architecture, from a Georgian dining room to a Jacobean wood-panelled gallery. The 7 individually decorated rooms are furnished with antiques and overlook the Minster, city walls and the gorgeous walled garden. Staff are very friendly and helpful. There is also an excellent restaurant, **Duel**. Rates include a delicious breakfast but not parking.

£££ Cedar Court Grand Hotel, Station Rise, T01904-380038, www.cedarcourt grand.co.uk. In an impressively grand landmark Edwardian building, a former railway HQ, this sumptuous 5-star has many facilities, including a pool, sauna, steam room, gym and treatment rooms. The luxurious rooms have marble bathrooms, espresso makers, fluffy bathrobes, flatscreen TVs, free Wi-Fi and Molton Brown toiletries. Rooms are **££££** including use of the spa. Parking in the nearby NCP, valet parking offered. Free Wi-Fi.

£££ The Golden Fleece, 16 Pavement, T01904-627151, www.thegoldenfleece york.co.uk. A few lovely rooms in a historic

pub, it's also extraordinarily well located with views of the Minster and the Shambles. Best of all, every inch of the place is said to be haunted. Breakfast is included. Parking in an NCP car park, a few mins' walk away.

£££ The Grange Hotel, 1 Clifton, T01904-644744, www.grangehotel.co.uk. This grand old building dating from the early 19th century has large, beautiful rooms with all modern amenities along with friendly staff and some of the best restaurants in York. It's well located in easy walking distance of the city centre. Free parking.

£££ Judges Lodging Hotel, 9 Lendal, T01904-638733, www.judgeslodgings york.co.uk. A short stroll from the Minster in a listed Georgian townhouse on the tourist track. Many of its rooms have 4-poster beds and some have views of the Minster.

£££ Royal York Hotel, Station Parade, T01904-653681, www.royalyorkhotel.co.uk. Makes, if nothing else, a lovely view, with three acres of landscaped gardens. It is designed to pamper in historic elegance. Facilities include a restaurant, bar, pool, gym, sauna and steam room.

££ Alhambra Court Hotel, 31 St Mary's, Bootham, T01904-628474, www.alhambracourthotel.co.uk. Well-appointed rooms with some period furnishings within walking distance of the centre. Free parking.

££ Bootham Guesthouse, 56 Bootham Cres, T01904-672123, www.bootham guesthouse.co.uk. A friendly, quiet place tucked inside a period building, only a few mins' walk from the centre, with cheery owners and hearty breakfasts. Free Wi-Fi and parking.

££ Bronte Guesthouse, 22 Grosvenor Terr, T01904-621066, www.bronte-guesthouse.com. In a period building with charming en suite rooms, within walking distance of the centre. Free parking. Breakfast included.

££ The Fort, 1 Little Stonegate, T01904-620222, www.thefortyork.co.uk. Centrally located characterful hostel with individually decorated 6-bed dorms and several doubles. Set above a bar, **Kennedy's**, it can be noisy, but it's good value, being at the lower end of this price range. Free Wi-Fi, luggage storage and tea and coffee.

££ Friar's Rest Guesthouse, 81 Fulford Rd, T01904-629823, www.friarsrest.co.uk. Has 7 rooms (bathroom en suite) 10 mins' walk from the centre along the river. Free parking and Wi-Fi.

££ Wheatlands Lodge Hotel, 75-85 Scarcroft Rd, T01904-654318, www.wheatlandslodge.co.uk. A large, friendly family-run place 5 mins' walk from the train station with all the modern conveniences, along with a pleasant bar and handy restaurant. Breakfast included. Free parking.

🍴 Restaurants

York p18, map p20
It seems like the only thing there's more of than churches in York is restaurants. Choose carefully from the ranks, and you can have a very good meal here.

££ Blue Bicycle, 34 Fossgate, T01904-673990, www.thebluebicycle.com. This fantastic restaurant serves fabulous gourmet dishes with a seafood emphasis in a gorgeous building that once served as a brothel. Don't even think about going if you haven't booked, though. Prices are at the top end of this price range.

££ Café Concerto, 21 High Petergate, T01904-610478, wwwcafeconcerto.biz. Daily 0830-2200. Creative fusion cuisine at this sunny, informal café-cum-bistro, with its walls papered with sheet music. It's good for a piece of cake and a coffee in the afternoon or an intimate dinner in the evening.

££ Café No 8, 8 Gillygate, T01904-653074, www.cafeno8.co.uk. Smart bistro serving top-notch food, using local ingredients where

possible. There's also a small attractive garden backing on to the city walls for outdoor dining.

££ The Grange Hotel, see page 32. Closed Sun evening. Modern European dishes in an unashamedly posh atmosphere. Prices are unsurprisingly steep at both its restaurants.

££ Melton's Too, 25 Walmgate, T01904-629222, www.meltonstoo.co.uk. Great bistro-style bar and restaurant and a good option for an excellent dinner or just an afternoon nibble. Offers modern dishes, with an emphasis on seasonal, local produce, in a 1690s building. Great value set menu (£13 for 3 courses, £11.50 for 2) available before 1900.

££ El Piano, 15-17 Grape La, T01904-610676, www.el-piano.com. Mon-Sat 1100-2300, Sun 1200-2100. Long-established vegan restaurant and tapas bar. Dishes are influenced by Spain, Latin American and the Middle East, using gluten-free, organic and locally sourced ingredients.

££-£ Goji, 36 Goodramgate, T01904-622614, gojicafe.co.uk. Mon- Fri 1100-1630, Sat 0900-1700, Sun 0900-1630, restaurant Fri-Sat 1830-2300. Vegetarian deli, café and restaurant serving great food including breakfast at weekends, homemade soup and cakes, with vegan options. Also sells excellent takeaway food and organic bread. 10% student discount.

£ Il Paradiso del Cibo, 40 Walmgate, T01904-611444, ilparadisodelcibo.com. Mon-Sat 1230-1500 and 1800-2200, Sun open from mid-Mar. Unpretentious, no-frills Italian eatery serving authentic homemade pasta and pizza at great prices.

£ Pig & Pastry, 35 Bishopsthorpe Rd, T01904-675115. Closed Sun. Great little deli and café popular with locals, just outside the tourist-filled centre. Try the eggs benedict followed by a slice of one of their homemade cakes. Gets very busy though so you may well end up sharing a table.

York p18, map p20
Some of York's pubs are almost too historic and quaint. You feel like it's a put on.
Ackhorne, 9 St Martins La, off Micklegate, T01904-671421. Great little real ale pub, tucked away off the main drag, offering a warm welcome and a good selection of beer to a mostly local clientele.
Black Swan, Peasholme Green, T01904-679131, www.blackswanyork.com. This place is one of York's quaint pubs. In a distinguished medieval timber-frame house, the pub dates back to 1417. Understandably, it is believed to be haunted, so look out for a filmy but beautiful girl staring anxiously into the fireplace.
Blue Bell, 53 Fossgate, T01904-654904. ~For friendly locals head to this tiny and adorable Edwardian pub where 2 dinky rooms (including the Smoke Room at the back) surround the little bar. The amiable staff will look out for you, there's good cask ale. Bar snacks only, including local cheeses and pork pies.
Lamb and Lion, High Petergate, T0845-460 9040, www.lambandlionyork.com. This Georgian townhouse pub next to Bootham Bar gate and in the shadow of the Minster has bags of character, roaring fires and good pub food. The beer garden is right up against the medieval city walls. They also have some well-appointed rooms (**£££**).
York Tap, train station, T01904-659009, www.yorktap.com. Choose from a wide selection of cask beers in this elegantly restored Victorian bar in the station.
Yorkshire Terrier Inn, 10 Stonegate, T01904-676722. No-frills pub owned by the York Brewery (www.york-brewery.co.uk) serving great ales and basic food. There's a brewery shop at the front of the building.

York p18, map p20
Cinema
City Screen Picturehouse, 13-17 Coney St, T0871 902 5726, www.picturehouses.co.uk. Part of the Picturehouse chain, showing latest release, arthouse and independent films in a riverside setting with a posh café and bar packing them in every night.
Reel Cinema York, Odeon buildings, Blossom St, T01509-221155. For mainstream films.
Vue York, Clifton Moor Centre, Stirling Rd, T08712 240240, www.myvue.com. 12-screen cinema.

Theatre
Friargate Theatre, Lower Friargate, T01904-613000, ridinglights.org. Home to the Riding Lights Theatre Company, this studio theatre also stages performances from touring companies.
Grand Opera House, Cumberland St, T0844-871 3024, www.atgtickets.com/venues. Has a variety of productions including ballet, theatre, musicals and opera.
Theatre Royal, St Leonard's Pl, T01904-623568, www.yorktheatreroyal.co.uk. Musicals, pantos and mainstream theatre.

York p18, map p20
In many ways, this whole town is one big shopping centre. Major shopping streets include **Stonegate**, with its antique jewellery shops, toyshops, and woollens, **Coppergate**, with its high-street shops for clothing, **Lendal St** with its department stores and chain bookstores. Less high profile but more interesting are the designer and vintage clothing boutiques and quality art stores on **Grape Lane** and **Swine Gate**. For more touristy shops you can join the crowds in **The Shambles** and nearby **Newgate Market**.

York *p18, map p20*
Horse racing
York Racecourse, T01904-620911,
www.yorkracecourse.com. One of the
best-known horse racing tracks in the country
is just outside town, 1 mile from York train
station. By road, the A64 and A1036 will get
you there. On race days, a shuttle bus runs
every 20 mins from York Station. York
Racecourse dates back to 1731.

Walking tours
See Getting around, page 19.

York *p18, map p20*
Mid-Feb JORVIK Viking Festival sees the
streets of York filled with Vikings and
Viking-related staged battles, drama and
other events.
Mar York Literature Festival showcases
famous novelists, poets and other writers. See
www.yorkliteraturefestival.co.uk for details.
Jul York's Early Music Festival is justifiably
famous, and historically based musical groups
travel here from all over the world to perform.
See also www.ncem.co.uk.
Jul York Mystery Plays will next be held in
2014, on 13 and 20 Jul. See under Wagon
Plays on www.yorkmysteryplays.org for
more information.

York *p18, map p20*
Bus
National Express, T08717-818178,
www.nationalexpress.com, run direct services
from **London Victoria** (from 4 hrs 50 mins),
Birmingham 1 direct daily (3 hrs 30 mins),
Manchester (from 2 hrs 30 mins), **Leeds**
3 daily (45 mins), **Sheffield** 9 daily (2 hrs
5 mins). For further information contact
National Rail Enquiries T08457-484950,
www.nationalrail.co.uk.

Train
There are direct services to York from
London King's Cross (2 hrs), **Birmingham
New Street** (2 hrs), **Manchester** Piccadilly
and Oxford Rd stations (1 hr 30 mins), **Leeds**
(30 mins) and **Sheffield** (45 mins).

Around York *p29*
Bus
There's a **National Express** (see above)
service to **Thirsk** from York (1 bus a day,
2 hrs 40 mins), and local bus services to
nearby towns such as **Kilburn**, **Coxwold** and
Helmsley. Buses stop at the market place

York *p18, map p20*
Hospital York District Hospital, Wigginton
Rd, T01904-631313.

Contents

North York Moors

The stark beauty of the moors never fails to impress. Were there no signs at all telling you that you had reached them, you would still know that you were there. The view changes from emerald green farmland to the dark, almost black-green hue of the heather. In summer, when it is in flower, the vista is tinted dark pink as far as the eye can see. At the farthest points of the North York Moors, you can drive for miles without seeing anything but roaming sheep, which, occasionally, you must shoo from the road in order to continue on your way. The villages here tend to be small and quaint and in the middle of nowhere. The names of villages – Goathland and Hutton-le-Dale – reflect the languages of centuries of invaders and there is a comfortable sense here that little has changed, or will change, as the decades go by.

Visiting the North York Moors → For listings, see pages 48.

Getting there and around

The Moorsbus, T01845-597000, www.northyorkmoors.org.net, connects many of the towns, in its brief operating season, otherwise a car is absolutely necessary to get to the smaller villages. Run by the National Park Authority, and intended to make the very limited transport through the region more convenient, the Moorsbus runs throughout the North York Moors in the high season. The service is very limited, operating only Sunday and bank holidays from Easter to late October. Still, it is helpful if you can arrange your schedule around it. You can pick up timetables in all area tourist offices. All-day tickets are £6 for an inner zone ticket and £9 for the outer zone. Up to four children travel free with a fare-paying adult except on the Arriva services 5 and 93, when they have to pay £1 each. Combined bus and train tickets (Moorslink) are also available. The all-day tickets give discounts fo up to 25% off sights and in some shops and restaurants.

For journey planning on buses, see the **Traveline Yorkshire** website, www.yorkshiretravel.net, or T0871-200 2233. There are also long-distance services to Beverley, Darlington, Hartlepool, Hull, Middlesbrough, Northallerton, Redcar, Saltburn, Scarborough, Stockton, Thirsk and York. ▸▸ *See Transport, page 48.*

Tourist information

See the North York Moors National Park website for general information: www.northyorkmoors.org.uk. There are two main national park information centres, in Danby (T01439-772737) and Sutton Bank, on the A170 east of Thirsk (T01845-597426). There are many tourist information centres throughout the park, which are helpful for all your questions about how to get around, things to see in the area and where to stay. They sell books, maps and guides for walks in the moors. There are also village information points in Goathland, Grosmont, Hutton Le Hole, Osmotherley, Rosedale Abbey and Thornton Le Dale.

North York Moors National Park (West)

Osmotherley

The little stone village of Osmotherley sits with medieval charm about 10 miles north of Thirsk. Once an agrarian centre, it is now best known to ramblers who wander by it while hiking the ambitious Cleveland Way. Even if you're more into four-wheel transport, it's worth a visit, both for its sheer cuteness and for its mysterious stone table. According to lore, John Wesley preached from atop this rock, although there's not much to back that up. There's also an old market cross nearby to glance at before you head for the Mount Grace Priory nearby. Well-marked walks from here include one to the priory (about 2 miles), or you can try your legs at the stretch of the **Cleveland Way** walk to the 299 m summit of **Scarth Wood Moor** and on to **Cod Beck Reservoir** about 3 miles away. Of course, if you think that's for wimps, you can get on the **Lyke Wake Walk**, which stretches for 42 exhausting miles across the rolling moors to the white cliffs of **Ravenscar** on the coast (see page 56).

Most people choose the short route to **Mount Grace Priory** ⓘ *T01609-883494, www.english-heritage.org.uk, Apr-Sep daily 1000-1800, Oct daily 1000-1700, Nov-Mar Sat-Sun 1000-1600, £5.20, under-16s £3.10, accessible on foot or car, just off the A19*, and for good reason. Its simple structure and lovely setting make it a uniquely beautiful place. Historians consider it to be the most important and best-preserved Carthusian ruin in Britain, and its modest structure stands in stark contrast to the more spectacular Cistercian ruins, such as Rievaulx (see page 41). Built in 1398, its simple design is explained by the equally simple life led by Carthusian monks, who lived lives of solitude – having taken vows of silence – unlike the communal Cistercians. Rather than living in grand shared houses, each Carthusian monk was given his own stone hut and a garden to tend, with a handsome church (the tower of which still remains) in the middle of the large grounds. Despite their proximity to one another, they lived in isolation – even their little homes were hidden from one another by tall stone walls. While most of the huts lie in ruins, one has been reconstructed to give an idea of their size and appearance. Two new rooms have also been opened, restored in style of the Arts and Crafts movement. The monastery was converted into a country house in the late 19th century, with William Morris carpets and wallpaper, which still survive today. Outside there's a herb garden, landscaped to fit the monks' descriptions of their own gardens. There's an on-site information centre and a gift shop.

Coxwold

The sweet little village of Coxwold, with its quaint stone buildings and flowering window boxes, has been attracting tourists for as long as the writer Laurence Sterne has been dead. Sterne, author of *The Life and Opinions of Tristam Shandy*, served as vicar at the church of St Michael's from 1760 until he died in 1768, and is buried in the churchyard. There's a stone on the porch from his first grave in London. Sterne's story is a strange one. Educated as a vicar, his writings made him a star. *Tristam Shandy* was published in 1760, and after that he was a famous figure on the London scene. Further volumes of the tale only made him more famous. When he died in London of pleurisy in 1768, he was buried there. But controversy arose immediately as rumours circulated that his grave had been vandalized and his body stolen along with hundreds of others, and sold for medical research. The story circulated for centuries, and so, in 1969, his body was exhumed. When the coffin was removed from the grave, authorities found a mixture of bones and five skulls inside. One of the skulls was determined to be Sterne's, and it, along with the bones, was taken to Coxwold for reburial. Exactly what happened to Sterne, and whose heads that were buried with his, is not known for certain. The most likely explanation is that the graverobbers took the body before the headstone was carved, and did not know that they had stolen a famous man. Upon figuring out just what they'd done, they hurriedly refilled his coffin with whatever body parts they could find.

Along with the curiosity of Sterne's grave, Coxwold also offers the charms of **St Michael's Church**, with its unusual octagonal tower and medieval stained-glass windows. Up the road is Sterne's home, **Shandy Hall** ① *T01347-868465, www.laurence sternetrust.org.uk, house May-Sep Wed 1400-1630, Sun 1430-1630, gardens May-Sep daily except Sat 1100-1630, house and garden £4.50, child £2.25, garden only £2.50, child £1.25,* which has been converted into a museum to his life, filled with books and memorabilia. The aptly named home was where Sterne lived when he wrote the controversial *Tristam Shandy* and his travel tales, *A Sentimental Journey through France and Italy*.

You can meet other tourists for a beer and some lunch at the comely Fauconburg Arms pub on Main Street. It is named, by the way, after the husband of Oliver Cromwell's daughter Mary. The happy couple lived in a house at nearby **Newburgh Priory**, which was once a monastery founded in 1150. According to lore, Mary brought her father's body back to her house at the priory after it was exhumed from Westminster Abbey in retaliation for Cromwell's leadership role in the Civil War. This story maintains that she brought only the body, and not the head (in order to conceal his identity), and then buried the parts she had at the priory. There's nothing much to back the story up, but it's a colourful tale nonetheless.

Byland Abbey

① *2 miles south of A170 between Thirsk and Helmsley, T01347-868614, www.english-heritage.org.uk. Apr-Sep daily 1000-1800, Oct-Mar Sat-Sun 1000-1600. £4.40, under-16s £2.60.*

There's not much left of the 12th-century Byland Abbey, but what remains looks like a Gothic sculpture. An arc of stone that once held a huge stained-glass window scoops the sky, and a single turret points up, as if indicating the direction of heaven. Surrounded by miles of nothing, the image is striking. For historians, its biggest attraction is the large section of cream-coloured medieval floor tile that remains in the chapel, continually threatened by the grass that tries to overgrow it. There's also a well-preserved walkway, believed to have been used by lay workers who served the cloistered monks.

Helmsley

Teetering at the edge of the North York Moors, Helmsley is a picture-perfect village, complete with flowering window boxes, stone cottages, arched bridges across streams, picturesque churchyards and the ruins of a Norman castle, in short, this town is a travel photo waiting to happen. Luckily, you're saved from the tooth-hurting cloyness of non-stop charm by the intercession of hundreds upon hundreds of tourists, and – that sure indication that a town is overrun – coach parking areas. There's a handy public car park in the central **town square**, which is an excellent starting base for an exploratory wander. The square is surrounded by shops and is the scene of the weekly market each Friday. The cross at the centre of the square marks the start of the **Cleveland Way** ⓘ *www.national trail.co.uk/clevelandway, or ask at the Helmsley tourist office or contact The Cleveland Way Project, T01439-770657, m.hodgson@northyorkmoors-npa.gov.uk.* The famed walking path that starts at Helmsley and crosses the North York Moors, the Cleveland Hills and the coastal cliffs before ending in Scarborough.

Beyond the square the town's medieval lanes are lined with twee shops likely to warm the heart of any grandmother. If you're looking for pink hand-knitted jumpers or garden gnomes, you'll be in heaven. Just past the shops, the stark ruins of **Helmsley Castle** ⓘ *T01439-770442, www.english-heritage.org.uk, Feb half term-Mar Sat-Sun 1000-1600, Apr-Sep daily 1000-1800, Nov-Feb Wed-Sun 1000-1300 and 1400-1600, £4.90, under-16s £2.90, entry includes audio tour, guided tours from mid-Jul to Sep at 1100 and 1330, £2.50,* overlook the town from a well-tended green field. While not a great deal is left of this Norman castle, what remains is quite evocative. You enter via a wooden bridge over the moat, past remnants of the walls. The one standing tower makes for a dramatic photo, while more recent 15th-century structures are also intact, and you can wander through them at will. There's an interactive exhibition in the Tudor mansion house and a model showing how the castle used to look.

At the edge of Helmsley is the 18th-century manor house **Duncombe Park** ⓘ *T01439-770213, www.duncombepark.com, Jun-Aug Sun-Fri 1100-1730, gardens and parkland £5, under-16s £3, parkland only £3, under-16s £2.* Built in 1713, the vast building sits on impressive grounds overlooking Helmsley Castle and the River Rye. It's the current home of Lord and Lady Feversham, the direct descendants of the Duncombe family who first ordered the house built in 1713. The house is closed to visitors but the 14 ha of landscaped gardens and 180 ha of wooded parkland are even more impressive. There's a spectacular view of Helmsley below.

Nunington Hall ⓘ *T01439-748283, www.nationaltrust.org, Jun-Aug 1330-1700 Tue-Sun, Mar-Oct Tue-Sun 1100-1700, Nov to mid-Dec Sat-Sun 1100-1600, £6.60, under-16s £3.30, joint ticket with Rievaulx Terrace and Temple (see below) £9.50, under-16s £5,* a grand 16th- and 17th-century manor house at the edge of the Rye, is most famous for its Carlisle Collection, a series of miniature rooms, all exquisitely filled with period furniture. The grand old house also features a sweeping staircase and lofty entrance hall. It's surrounded by lovely gardens and woods, and the whole place is said to be haunted, although you're more likely to see tourists than ghosts.

Rievaulx Abbey

ⓘ *T01439-798228, www.english-heritage.org.uk. Feb Sat-Sun 1000-1600, Apr-Sep daily 1000-1800, Jul-Aug daily 0930-1800, Oct daily 1000-1700, Nov-Jan 1000-1600 daily. £5.80, under-16s £3.50. There is a well-signposted walking path from Helmsley to Rievaulx (about 3 miles), otherwise you can take the Moorsbus in season, see page 38, or drive the brief distance following the clear signs that lead you there.*

Several miles from Helmsley, just inside the North York Moors, are the remains of one of the most spectacular abbeys in all of England. Once the most important Cistercian abbey in the country, Rievaulx was founded in 1132 by French Cistercians seeking to expand their sect into Britain. Its biggest period of growth came under the rule of its third abbot, St Aelred about 20 years later, when construction first began on most of the buildings that remain now. Aelred was the most famous monk of his day, and he is considered by some to have been the greatest religious writer in England during the Middle Ages. For several hundred years, Rievaulx was an enormous working abbey, with farmland, fisheries, textiles and mining operations run by lay workers. At its peak, Rievaulx was home to 140 choir monks and 500 lay brothers and lay servants. From the 13th century on, however, the population in the abbey declined, as political changes made it difficult for the abbey to prosper. By the time Rievaulx was suppressed in 1538, only 22 monks still lived on the grounds.

The ruins of Rievaulx are impressively complete, and the look of the place – with the jagged arched walls juxtaposed against green wooded hills – is breathtaking. Enough is left of the buildings to give an awe-inspiring indication of how magnificent it all must have been when it was complete. In particular, the spectacular **nave**, where arch within symmetrical arch still stand, is vast and towering. Signs tucked into the grass and mounted on the walls show where the chapel stood, and what the various rooms that remain once were. Little is left of the cloister, but the Chapter House still holds a shrine to the first abbot. There's also a well-preserved **refectory**, considered one of the finest ever built by the Cistercians. Even the monks' **dormitory** and **latrine** remain.

The on-site **visitor centre** offers more information about Rievaulx, as well as a few sandwiches and drinks. The little village around the abbey – with medieval stone houses – is simultaneously charming and forbidding, the latter, perhaps, simply because of the rural isolation of the place.

On the wooded hill above Rievaulx, are the terraced woodlands that once made up some of the gardens of Duncombe Park. The **Rievaulx Terrace and Temple** ① *T01439-748283, www.nationaltrust.org.uk, med-Feb to Oct daily 1100-1700, £5.20, under-16s £2.95, joint ticket with Nunnington Hall (see above) £9.50, under-16s £5*, is separate from the abbey, divided by thick woods. The grass-covered terraces and woods were designed in the mid-1700s to offer a bird's eye view of the abbey, as it still does today. There are two elaborate 'temples' on the terrace, with period furnishings and paintings. There is also an ongoing display on landscape design.

North York Moors National Park (East)

Hutton-le-Hole

Hutton-le-Hole is undeniably precious, with perfect stone cottages and colourful gardens framing a quiet stream with grassy banks upon which lovers woo and children gambol. Pesky sheep wander the streets at will, stealing a nibble through fence posts, and snoozing in the shade of garden walls. But everybody knows about this place, so it's packed to the gills with tourists and in such a little village, the crowds can be downright oppressive. The locals who run the *Barn Guesthouse and Tearoom* and the *Crown* pub try to keep up, but are quickly overwhelmed and then submerged in the waves of hungry and thirsty travellers. As these are the only options for food and drink, it would not be a bad decision to see Hutton-le-Hole and then go eat somewhere else. Still, it's charming, and worth a quick wander. Its proximity to Helmsley, just 8 miles away, is probably as responsible for its popularity as are its pretty gardens.

Along with the sheer charm of the place, the **Ryedale Folk Museum** ① *T01751-417367, www.ryedalefolkmuseum.co.uk, daily 1000-1630, closed 9 Dec-20 Jan, £7, under-16s £6, family £22.50*, is the biggest draw in town. This five-acre museum is respected for its efforts to recreate and preserve historic rural life. Inside you can watch metal being hammered in a 16th-century blacksmith's shop, and glass being blown in a glass furnace. There's a traditional herb farm, a Tudor cottage, craft workshops, a gallery and that's just the start. The museum's gift shop has information on the area and on local walks for amblers.

Lastingham

After only a mile or so of sheep and moors and winding narrow roads, the tiny hilltop village of Lastingham appears with its stern stone houses whose gloomy aspect is successfully lightened by the colour spilling from lush gardens and windowboxes. In the summer, moors sheep wander down the curving roads and graze lazily in the picturesque churchyard around the parish church. In fact, you tend to inadvertently herd the docile creatures while seeking out the more interesting gravestones. (In revenge, you can eat them for lunch at the pleasant **Blacksmiths Arms** pub directly opposite.) Lastingham is tiny enough and far enough off the beaten track to be one of those rare lovely Yorkshire villages not overrun with day-tripping tourists.

Along with the almost clichéd perfection of the town, the main attraction here is **St Mary's Church**, which holds the distinction of having one of the oldest crypts in the country. The small sanctuary is pleasant, if somewhat ordinary, because of repeated renovations over the centuries, but the crypt is simply extraordinary. Bede mentioned a monastery at Lastingham in 731 in his *History of the English Church and People*, and it's believed that the first monastery was founded here more than a hundred years before that. It was started by a bishop named Cedd, who later died in Lastingham of the plague in 664, and was buried here. This made the church a regular stopping point for pilgrims. Vikings destroyed much of the church in the ninth century, but it was rebuilt a century later as a shrine to St Cedd (who, by then, had been beatified). All of the crypt that doesn't date from the 600s was built then. (The crypt is thought to be the only one in England with an apse (rounded end) together with a chancel, nave and side aisles.) The four Norman columns supporting the vault have bases that appear to be of pre-Conquest workmanship. Historians believe that the crypt has not been changed since the time of William the Conquerer. Best of all, access is free, and it's not unusual to have the whole place to yourself.

Rosedale

It's best to approach Rosedale from the north, as from that direction you top a high hill with an extraordinary view of rolling moors that extends for miles. From a distance the old mining village is obscured by trees, and thus it appears suddenly in front of you as you drive up. It's a less charming and more gangly town than Lastingham or Hutton-le-Hole, where nature seems to be taking over; no sheep wander its streets keeping the grass tidy, houses are hidden away behind thick foliage. Built as it is on the side of a steep hill, in places its streets are precipitously vertical, and the signs telling you where to find **Rosedale Abbey** are hard to see, and difficult to understand. If you do successfully find your way to the town – which took its deceptive name from a long-gone Cistercian monastery – you'll find there's not much there except for the beautiful countryside. The remains of the abbey were largely scavenged to build **St Lawrence's** parish church. Still, the crowds pour in to Rosedale village on summertime weekends, some to head out on one of several **walks** that pass by the area. A particularly daunting one follows the route of the old moorland railway that once carried ore mined from the nearby hills. The train line is now a popular pathway offering extraordinary views. Bear in mind, of course, that the sweeping views are directly proportional to the steepness of the path. You can join the walk at **Hill Cottages**, about a mile or so north of Rosedale Abbey (a OS Landranger 100 map is recommended). A full walk around the head of the valley covers 10 largely uphill miles and takes several hours. There are a few small inns in town, as well as the inevitable **Abbey Tea Room**, and a caravan site down by the river.

Pickering

One of the biggest market towns in the moors, Pickering, like Helmsley, is a hub of sorts. Although it's a rather charmless town, it offers lots of places to stay, impressive castle ruins, and, of course, the fabulous **North Yorkshire Moors Railway**. It makes a good base for wandering the eastern moors by car, foot or via the episodic Moorsbus or the romantic steam railway. There's usually parking places to be found in the centre of town, although if that fails there are car parks down near the railyard. Near the centre of the hillside town is the gloomy **Church of St Peter and St Paul**. The church features a Norman font, and is famous (or infamous) for the 15th-century wall paintings in its nave, which were painted over in the 19th century by an overly anxious vicar who feared they would arouse passion and idolatry among his parishioners. Later restored, they tell biblical and historical tales, but hardly arouse passion or idolatry.

Further up the hill from the church are the solid stone walls of **Pickering Castle** ① T01751-474989, www.english-heritage.org.uk, daily Apr-Sep 1000-1800, £3.90, under-16s £2.30. Once a splendid royal home used primarily as a hunting lodge, the castle dates back to William the Conquerer, although most of what remains was built in the 12th century. The motte (a man-made hill on which the keep was built) was ordered built by William himself, in order that he could defend the castle from attacks coming from the surrounding territory. His 11th-century defences make for excellent 21st-century views – from the top you can see for miles. Aside from the walls and the motte, there's not much left of the castle, but what remains is impressive. The restored castle chapel was built in 1227, and features an exhibition on the history of the structure, including the fact that Richard II was held captive here after his abduction.

You can see the steam from the undeniably pretty **North Yorkshire Moors Railway** ① 12 Park St, T01751-472508, www.nymr.co.uk, £14-£24 for an all-day adult pass, depending on the area covered, under-16s £7-12, over-60s £12-21, £28-48 for a family of 6, engines from the top of the castle's motte. A short walk downhill takes you to the quaint station, which, right down to the advertisement posters on the walls, has been restored to look as it did in 1937. This is what most people are in Pickering to see, and if you come across no tourists elsewhere in town, you will surely find plenty on the colourful train platform, where the crowd surges forward to see the old engines pull in, puffing mightily, in an utterly authentic swirling cloud of steam and cinders. The train takes an 18-mile journey from Pickering to Grosmont, stopping along the way at Levisham Station in the scenic Newton Dale Valley, then at Newton Dale Halt and Goathland Station. The train is particularly popular with walkers, as a variety of paths pass near those stations, so you can easily leave the train at one stop and walk to the next. For route details, you can download basic PDFs from the NYMR website (see above) or order a book from their online shop. Alternatively, see the online shop at www.northyorkmoors.org.uk.

The whole enterprise is a labour of love, since most of the workers on the trains and in the stations are volunteers. Even the old carriages, with their wooden fittings, were restored by volunteers working in their spare time. The train follows one of the oldest lines in England; trains travelled this route from 1835 to 1965. After being closed down, the line was reopened as a private operation in 1973. Days and times of operation vary from month to month, although service is hourly during the summer. Timetables can be picked up at the station or at any TIC in the area, or see the website.

In a fine Regency building behind the train station, the **Beck Isle Museum of Rural Life** ① *T01751-473653, www.beckislemuseum.org.uk, Feb-Oct daily 1000-1700, £5.50, under-16s £3*, has a series of 27 rooms devoted to different aspects of historical life in the area, including a cobblers, a barber's shop, a blacksmith's forge and a wheelwright. Or you could just taste a little rural life of your own at the **Pickering Trout Lake** ① *Newbridge Rd, T01751-474219, www.pickeringtroutlake.co.uk, Feb half term and late Mar-Oct daily 1000-1900 (or dusk if earlier), £6 per rod*, next to the station, where, in a kind of circular food chain, you can either catch fish to eat, or throw food for the fish to eat. You can hire tackle and bait, as well as fish food, on site.

Thornton-le-Dale

Just two miles from Pickering, the village of Thornton-le-Dale would have you believe it's the 'prettiest village in Yorkshire'. Unfortunately, that's just not the case. It's pretty enough, but when it comes to sheer sweetness and beauty, Lastingham and Lealholm leave it in the dust. Still, it's worth a look. Its stone houses and old market cross are attractive, and it has interesting long houses. The man-made streams that babble down the main roads are a remnant of its past as a milltown. The old stocks have place of honour next to the cross in the village centre. Just across the street from the cross are **Lady Lumley's Almshouses**, a series of 12 structures built in 1670, and still used as housing. The old **forge** has been converted into a twee gift shop, and its old pharmacy into a modern chemist. Inevitably there's a glut of teashops here, all of which you can give a miss without any guilt. Its main claim to fame is its one thatch-roofed cottage, which tourists crowd to photograph.

Dalby Forest

① *Visitor centre T01751-460295, daily 1000-1600, May-Sep open until 1700. Cars £7, £4 after 1600, Nov-Feb £4. See also www.forestry.gov.uk.*

Just outside Thornton-le-Dale, the Dalby Forest begins. A favourite with hikers and cyclists, the thick expanse of wilderness includes a number of paths and cycle routes. The most popular walks pass near the car park at **Low Stain Dale**; the best known of these is the **Bridestones Trail** which features many of the mysterious sandstone boulders that appear throughout the moors, and whose origin is not really known. There are a number of well-marked routes to choose; see the website above for details. If you'd rather drive, there's a nine-mile road through the forest (above fee applies) that ends near the town of Hackness. Whichever way you travel, it's a good idea to visit the visitor centre, at **Low Dalby** (see above), where you can get information on trails, wildlife and the history of the forest. There's also a restaurant and play area here.

Also in the forest is the treetop adventure course **Go Ape** ① *Low Dalby, goape.co.uk, £30, 10-17 year olds £24, open Feb-Nov*, with all the usual zip wires, rope walks and tummy-flipping views of the Vale of Pickering. They also have an hour-long Forest Segway Experience, where you can explore forest trails on a two-wheel electric segway, a bit like a child's scooter with thick wheels at the sides.

Levisham and Lockton

Just at the edge of the Dalby Forest, you can pick up the North Yorkshire Moors Railway at Levisham Station, which is about a mile outside the pretty flower-strewn village of Levisham. A popular **walk** passes through here as well, heading to the equally charming town of Lockton about a mile away, where there is a handy youth hostel; see page 48. (Be aware that it is a very long mile, as the two villages are separated by a deep gorge.) Both villages are so old that they are mentioned in the *Domesday Book*. For many people though, the longest walk they will take is the short walk from the station to the **Horseshoe Inn** (see page 48), which does an excellent lunch. It has a few rooms as well although, if you haven't booked in advance, you'll have to be satisfied with a meal. Still, few things in life are more pleasant than sitting in front of the Horseshoe on a sunny day watching the weary walkers stride by.

Hole of Horcum

This extraordinary gorge just off the A169 north of Levisham is so breathtaking that local officials had a car park built opposite it to stop motorists running one another off the road as they gazed at it. A deep, heather-covered indentation in the hills, much lore surrounds the Hole, which is also called the Devil's Punchbowl. Legend holds, for instance, that a giant named Wade scooped the Hole when he grabbed a handful of dirt to throw at his wife during one of their rows. The clod missed her, and fell a mile away, forming the hill known as **Blakey Topping**. The view from the edge is stunning, also a number of paths lead down into the depths of the valley, and across to the nearby hills.

Goathland

If you feel like you've seen this place before – with its plain stone houses, bright red roofs and close-cropped village green – you probably have. The town of Goathland stood in for the imaginary 'Aidensfield' in the popular 1960s TV series *Heartbeat*.

The town's name sounds like Goatland but it's actually a corruption of the word 'gaut', which meant 'gorge'. 'Sheepland' might be a more appropriate name, since farmers have grazing rights to the whole town, and sheep wander freely, grazing on the wide lawns, keeping the village green sheared down nearly to dirt, and nibbling naughtily at flowers in people's gardens. While the town is distinctive – all stone cottages with unusual red roofs – most of the attraction lies in natural wonders at the edge of the village. Carved by the movement of water, Goathland is surrounded by natural water features, including several waterfalls. The best of the bunch is the impressive 21-m **Mallyan Spout**, which can be reached by a footpath that starts next to the **Mallyan Spout Hotel**, see page 48. You can also pick up the **North Yorkshire Moors Railway** here, and take a ride courtesy of steam power. From Goathland you can also hike up to the tiny village of **Beck Hole**, accessible only by foot. The mini-village features an equally small pub, the **Birch Hall Inn**, which is highly rated by pub experts. It also serves as a store and sandwich shop, and its locally made pies and stotties (flatcake sandwiches) are legendary.

Around Grosmont

Several miles of lovely moorland northeast of Goathland, the village of Grosmont bustles in the summertime, with traffic from trains, coaches and the Moorsbus unloading crowds of walkers attracted to the excellent walking paths in the area. But, aside from the **North Yorkshire Moors train** station, where the steam engines are lined up at the end of every day (Grosmont is the terminus), there's not much to see in the town itself. Built to house workers on the old Pickering-Whitby train line, the town is plain and utilitarian. Similarly, the nearby towns of **Egton** and **Danby** are popular primarily for their lovely natural settings, and as stops for walkers making their way down one of the many moors paths. Egton, and its neighbour **Egton Bridge**, has historic religious attraction as well. Known as 'the village missed by the Reformation' Egton Bridge remained a staunchly Catholic stronghold throughout the suppression of Catholicism. It was the birthplace of Father Nicholas Postgate, who carried on a secret Catholic ministry in the town, and was arrested in 1678 for illegally baptizing a child. After his trial in York, the 80-year-old priest was hanged, drawn and quartered. The Egton Bridge **Church of St Hedda** holds a number of Postgate's belongings. On a walking path midway between Egton and Egton Bridge is the **Mass House**, which still has a tiny chapel secreted away in its loft, where once-banned Catholic masses were held. The loft, which is accessible only by a hidden passageway, had been forgotten until it was discovered in the mid-19th century.

Lealholm

Despite other claims to the contrary, it is entirely possible that this is the prettiest village in Yorkshire. A few miles northeast of Grosmont on a narrow country lane, the town appears as the road dips down into a small valley. Thick green trees surround the cottages gathered at the edge of the shallow River Esk. There really is nothing here at all, except for the rare simple beauty of the place. The river is crossed downstream by a bridge of peach-tinged stone, while a short stroll away a stepping stone bridge in the same subtle pastel hue offers a more amusing way to cross from one bank to the other. Nearby, you might see a child being taught to fish by his grandfather, and residents catching up on their gardening may pass you with arms filled with plant cuttings. You get the feeling that the quiet here is constant. Only a handful of buildings make up the centre of town, including the cosy Board Inn, which has a few rooms and a good restaurant. Virtually all of the houses in this farming village have the same enigmatic symbol above their doors, and some bear the inscription, 'Ancient Society of Shepherds'.

North York Moors listings

● **Where to stay**

Helmsley *p40*

If you're looking to stay in Helmsley, there is no shortage of accommodation, as long as you don't mind the B&B variety. Many B&Bs line Ashdale Rd (just up Bondgate from the square). If you prefer a hotel, there are fewer options, though one of the best is the slightly expensive **££££ Feversham Arms Hotel**, just behind the old church, 1 High St, T01439-770766, www.fevershamarmshotel.com. Upmarket hotel with spa, outdoor pool and luxurious rooms. There is an excellent bar and restaurant as well. Room rates include room service breakfast and use of the spa.

£££ Black Swan, Market Pl, T01439-770466, www.blackswan-helmsley.co.uk. Lovely walled garden, pub and restaurant (**£££-££**) offering stylish rooms.

£ YHA Helmsley, Carlton La, T0845-371 9638, www.yha.org.uk. Good budget choice.

Hutton-le-Hole *p42*

££ Barn Guest House, T01751-417311, www.barnguesthouse.com. Good-value accommodation but usually booked months in advance in the summertime.

Pickering *p44*

In the summer, accommodation in Pickering can get booked up quickly.

£££ White Swan Inn, Market Pl, T01751-472288, www.white-swan.co.uk. The best place to stay in Pickering has individually designed rooms, invitingly named as 'hideaway', 'treat' or 'vintage'. The pub has open fires and there's a smart restaurant serving superb food. Free Wi-Fi.

Campsites

Spiers House Campsite, Cropton Forest, T0845-130 8224, campingintheforest.co.uk. A wooded site owned by the Forestry Commission on the edge of the national park. There are also cabins to rent (see forestholidays.co.uk).

Levisham and Lockton *p46*

££ Horseshoe Inn, T01751-460213, www.horshoelevisham.co.uk. Comfortable rooms and a warm welcome in this village pub on the moors. Hearty Yorkshire fare (**££**) served in the pub with open fires.

£ YHA Dalby Forest, T0845-371 9128, www.yha.org.uk. In Lockton, near Levisham station, this hostel is in a former school.

Goathland *p46*

££ Mallyan Spout, T01947-896486, www.mallyanspout.co.uk. Superb views over the Esk Valley, charming rooms with flatscreen TVs and room service, and a good restaurant (**££**). Free Wi-Fi.

Camping

La Rosa, see La Rosa Hotel, page 65. Just as quirky as **La Rosa Hotel** in Whitby, this eco-friendly campsite between Goathland and Egton prides itself on its green credentials with compost loos and candles. It also offers vintage caravans, a tipi to rent and a cosy Swallow Barn, sleeping 2 (**£££**).

● **Transport**

Helmsley *p40*
Bus

There is a bus service between Helmsley and other nearby towns including York and Scarborough, as well as the **Moorsbus** (see page 38) which runs a weekly service from late Mar to late Oct.

Contents

Footprint features

Coastal Yorkshire

From the edge of the moors you can look into the distance and see the deep blue – almost midnight blue – of the North Sea. The black-purple hills roll right to the edge of land, and the sudden appearance of the flat expanse of sea is almost startling. Here the atmosphere changes drastically from the straightforward farm communities to the wry humour of the wayfarers who make their living at sea. Mysterious moorland stones give way to mischievous whalebone sculptures. The shrieking of gulls replaces the vibrato of sheep. Gentle hills are truncated by threatening cliffs. Similarly, the stolid stone villages of the moors disappear, and colourful towns like Scarborough, with its creams and yellows, Whitby, with its blue and russet hues, and Robin Hood's Bay, with its vivid red rooftops, gleam. This is a different Yorkshire in many ways, but the seaside promenades, rock candy and silly hats are also accompanied by ancient ruins of castles and abbeys that tell the tale of the history of this land.

Visiting Coastal Yorkshire

Getting around

It's relatively difficult to travel around by **train**, as only Scarborough and Whitby have stations. Trains to Scarborough run from Hull every 1½ hours, and from York every 45 minutes. There are four trains daily to Whitby from Danby, Grosmont and Middlesbrough. The North York Moors Railway, see page 44, links Whitby and Pickering.

A series of coastal **roads** skirt the ocean and connect to one another, the A174 in the north, the A171 in the centre and the A165 in the south. Keep an eye out for signs, as many towns along the coast have only one entrance road and if you miss it, you've missed it. There are regular **buses** between Scarborough and Helmsley, Hull, Leeds, Milton, Middlesbrough, Pickering, Robin Hood's Bay and Whitby. For journey planning on buses, see the Traveline Yorkshire website, www.yorkshiretravel.net, or T0871-200 2233. For information on the periodic Moorsbus service, see page 35. ▸▸ *See Transport, page 69.*

The coast to Whitby

Staithes

The northernmost village on the Yorkshire coast, little Staithes clings tenaciously to the edge of the land. It's easy to miss the turnoff from the A174, so keep an eye out for the signs, and don't be put off by the first somewhat grim view of the town. After you park in the public car park and walk down the cliff to the town, you'll understand why you came this far. (Don't be tempted to drive into the town; the signs are true – you really can't park down there, and you don't even want to think about trying to turn a car around on its claustrophobically narrow streets.) It's a wonder this weatherbeaten town still exists, considering the strength of the storms that regularly slam against it. But it's a good thing that it hangs on, as Staithes is probably the most historically authentic fishing village in the region. In fact, it has changed little since Captain James Cook came here as a boy to bide his time before he could take to the sea. While some coastal towns are fairy-tale pretty, Staithes is rugged, yet not without charm. Set against the backdrop of the cliff known as **Cowbar Nab**, the village is divided down the middle by a deep gorge, and on either side are stone houses – some on the side of the steep divide seem to defy gravity – with red tiled roofs. Everywhere are fishing nets and lobster pots drying in the sun. Fishing and crabbing are still the main business here, and the small harbour is filled with bobbing, workaday boats – this is no yacht harbour. While the town has a look of unchanging completeness about it, in fact, many of its buildings have washed away over the years. The colourful **Cod and Lobster** pub has blown away three times. The grocer's shop near the pub, where James Cook worked as a lad, was destroyed by the weather in 1745 – the building now on the site (marked by a plaque) is a replacement.

To learn more about Captain Cook, head to the High Street for the **Captain Cook and Staithes Heritage Centre** ① *T01947-841454, www.captaincookatstaithes.co.uk, daily 1000-1700, Jan Sat-Sun only, £2.75, under-16s free*, which not only tells the story of his life, but includes a recreation of an 18th-century Staithes street, complete with shops. Otherwise, there's not much to do here except to wander around and take in the sights and sounds. Just north of town you can hike up the **Boulby Cliffs**, which tower at 200 m, making them the highest on the coast. Or you can follow the cars with surfboards sticking out the windows to the nearby beaches said to offer some of the best waves in England.

Kettleness and Goldsborough

The barren strip of rocky coast at Kettleness is often overlooked by travellers, and, in fairness, there's not much here except an amazing view. Once the site of massive alum mines, the clifftops here are empty of foliage, and only the tiny village and massive flocks of seabirds provide signs of life. It would seem you'd need wings to live here, and, in fact, the entire village was destroyed in a landslide in 1829 – the villagers were plucked from the sea by ships. Today the towering brown cliffs make for devastatingly stark photos and a fascinating hike. Half a mile from Kettleness, the town of Goldsborough stands on the site of a fourth-century Roman signal station. The road known as **Wade's Causeway** was once a Roman road. Still, this one is mainly for history buffs, as there's not much to see here now save for a grass-covered mound off the road between Kettleness and Goldsborough.

Whitby

Erstwhile home to both Bram Stoker and Captain Cook, Whitby is a town with two distinct personalities. The waterfront promenade with novelty shops, candy floss and fish and chip shops is one Whitby, while the other is manifested in the grim clifftop church and the skeletal abbey which loom above the town like an admonishment. This is one of the most interesting towns in all of Britain, a beautiful and paradoxical place. For centuries, Whitby was cut off from the rest of the country by its isolated location at the foot of cliffs. By the 18th century, however, it had become a prosperous major port and a northern leader in shipbuilding, fishing and whaling. Its wealth lasted through the 19th century and is demonstrated in the row of fine Georgian houses on the top of the west cliff, built by and for successful shipbuilders. Most of the town, though, is more modest, with the whitewashed cottages and humble shops built for fishermen making up the most common structures.

Arriving in Whitby

Getting there Whitby station is on the harbour near the town centre. Whitby is on the A174, and is well signposted. There are large **car** parks next to the train station. The bus station is next to the train station on Langborne Rd. ▶▶ *See Transport, page 69.*

Getting around The River Esk divides the town as it flows out to sea. This provides a handy geographical division of the town's two personalities: Whitby Abbey stands on the east cliff above the oldest section of Whitby, while a statue of Cook and a massive arch of whalebones dominate the more modern west side. The town is quite small, and best explored on foot. There are a very few local buses, with a stop near the train station, but these are only useful if you're going out of town, as walking is simply the best way to get around.

Tourist information Whitby TIC ① *corner of Langborne Rd and New Quay, near the bus station, T01723-383636, May-Jun 0930-1800, Jul-Sep 0930-1900, Oct-Apr daily 1000-1630.* It offers maps, information on tours, reduced price parking tickets and an accommodation and chalet booking service.

Eastern Whitby

As you cross the swing bridge toward eastern Whitby, looking out to sea the two piers on either side of the river reach out into the water like pincers, with a small lighthouse in the centre of each. Cobblestone streets that twist and turn up the eastern cliffside are flanked on either side by tourist-orientated shops, restaurants and pubs. Because there was limited space at the base of the cliffs, buildings were constructed very close together and they crowd up the steep sides of the hills, connected by medieval pedestrian alleyways (called ginnels) and stone staircases. **Church St** is the main route on this side, and it is filled with jewellery shops peddling Whitby jet – the famed glossy black stone (actually fossilized wood) that was so fashionable among the funereal set in Victorian times – antique stores and clothing shops.

Tiny **Grape Lane**, which branches off to the right, has buildings dating back to the 17th and 18th centuries. About midway down its short length is a former bank building with a single bottle-glass window that stretches the length of the building, the result of window tax evasion. Nearby is the former home of Captain John Walker, a ship owner under whom Captain Cook served his apprenticeship from 1746-49. The 17th-century house has been converted into the **Captain Cook Memorial Museum** ① *T01947-601900, www.cook museumwhitby.co.uk, mid-Feb to Mar 1100-1500, Apr-Oct 0945-1700 daily, Mar 1100-1500 Sat, Sun, £4.80, under-16s £3.30,* and contains a number of pieces of memorabilia, although some of it is only distantly related to Cook's life.

Dracula's town

The Irish author Bram Stoker was searching for a hit when he visited Whitby on holiday in 1893. He was working with Sir Henry Irving at the time, running the London Lyceum Theatre, and he longed to write a play that would bring attention to the theatre and to himself. Instead, of course, he ended up writing a novel that has continued to attract readers – and filmmakers – for more than a century.

Staying at No 6 Royal Crescent, Stoker was taken by the dark beauty of the town and its ruins. Searching for a villain, he discovered the name 'Dracula' while reading in the old Subscription Library near where Pier Road meets Khyber Pass. He based the Count's shipwreck arrival in Whitby – wherein his vessel crashes into the rocks near the pier – on an actual shipwreck that occurred here in 1885. He would later have one of the characters in the novel describe the abbey he could see from his own window as "a most noble ruin, of immense size, and full of beautiful and romantic bits". He placed the novel's heroines, Mina and Lucy, as well as Count Dracula's attorney, in houses on East Crescent. And describes the town in detail, as Mina races down the western cliff, across the bridge, up Church Street, then climbs the stairs to the churchyard in her bid to save her friend.

While there is certainly a kind of cult of *Dracula* in Whitby, and visitors could be forgiven for thinking the town cultivates this; in fact, the reverse is true. The town is not gloomy because Stoker based *Dracula* here. The feel of the place hasn't changed in centuries, and it seems entirely probable that if he had not based a horror novel here, somebody else would have.

The cobbled area at the intersection of Church and Grape streets was once the Tollgate where, until 1540, the abbot of Whitby gathered his dues. The **Salt Pan Well Steps** leading off Church St climb up to the old ropery which once made rigging for shipbuilders. Following the path to the **Boulby Bank** (once used by monks from the abbey to move goods down to the seafront) and past the old **Seamen's Hospital** leads to a gallery with wide views across the town and harbour. Nearby is **Elbow Terrace**, which once held a busy smuggler's tunnel, long ago filled in and replaced with houses. Back at the top of Church Street is the curved base of the famous **199 steps** up to the Gothic **St Mary's Church**. Bram Stoker memorialized the steps in his novel *Dracula*, in which Mina, in a frantic effort to save Lucy, rushes up the steps to the churchyard above. Climbing to the top is the equivalent of climbing an 11-storey building, so most people don't rush up; they creep, pausing to take in the view and grab a breath along the way. It's easy to see why the steps struck Stoker: they were originally built for pallbearers carrying coffins up to the churchyard at the top. It must have been a spectacularly dark sight, the black-clad people silently carrying a body up the long stairway as the church bell tolled. At night, the gloomy old church is lit by spotlights aimed up from the ground – the architectural equivalent of the old campground trick of holding a torch under your chin to cast scary shadows on your face. Local young people have discovered that if they stand in front of the lights and stretch their arms out to either side they can cast giant shadows that look, from the town, like moving crosses on the walls of the church – it's funny, in a scary way.

The windswept churchyard reaches to the very edge of the high seafront cliff and is almost too gloomy to be real, with long grass bending in the constant wind past the blackened tombstones. Hollywood could not create a spookier looking place. The Romanesque church dates back to the 12th century (although it has been altered many times since then), and the inside is even more strange than the outside. In the 18th century, the chapel was filled with wooden galleries and high-backed box pews that fill every inch of space. Some have the names of families painted distinctively on the side. One is labelled 'For strangers only'. The three-level pulpit is undoubtedly a matter of necessity: it has to be high in order for the vicar to be seen from the high-walled pews.

Through the churchyard to the back is a lane leading to **Whitby Abbey** ① *T01947-603568, www.english-heritage.org.uk, Apr-Sep 1000-1800, Oct Thu-Mon 1000-1700, Nov to Mar Sat-Sun 1000-1600, £6.20, under-16s £3.70, family £16.10, if the stairs are a problem, there is a car park at the top of the cliff behind the abbey, follow the brown signs off the A171, which is directly behind St Mary's.* Over the years, Whitby Abbey has been one of the most photographed ruins in the country, and it is an astonishingly bleak combination of terrain and architecture that can be seen from miles away. An abbey has stood here since the seventh century, when the Northumbrian king, Osway, first founded a monastery, unusually, one that was for both men and women, on this site. The abbey flourished under the leadership of the abbess Hild, later St Hild, and grew to be a religious centre in Anglo-Saxon society. It's believed that the monastery was destroyed by the Danes in the ninth century (the only remains of this first abbey are a handful of gravestones near the nave). The abbey was not rebuilt until after the Norman Conquest, when a knight named Reinfrid, who fought on the side of William the Conquerer at the Battle of Hastings, decided to rebuild it. The Benedictine abbey he founded here lasted until Henry VIII suppressed the country's monasteries. The land was sold to a wealthy family in the 17th century, who demolished much of the abbey and built the large manor house adjacent that is now the abbey's visitor centre. It is believed that the only reason the abbey ruins still stand is because its distinctive outline was an important navigation point for ships. The most impressive part of the structure that still remains is the 13th-century choir, with its soaring east wall and banks of arched windows. In the grass inside the choir are deep markings showing where the original church ended in a rounded apse. The 13th-century north transept stands at the site of the church's crossing, and still has a medieval inscription carved into its northern arcade column crediting a monk with carving a long lost altar. The first known poem in English, 'The Song of Creation', was written here by a monk named Caedmon.

Western Whitby

The western side of the town is mostly a 19th-century development, created when Whitby became a popular seaside resort, and the mood of holiday frivolity couldn't be more different from the town's east side. Along the waterfront all the usual noisy arcades, chip shops and 'kiss me quick' hats are present and accounted for. Further down Pier Road is the more serious attraction of the **RNLI Whitby Lifeboat Museum** ① *T01947-602001, Mar-Nov daily 1000-1700, Nov-Dec daily 1100-1600 and Jan-Mar Sat-Sun 1100-1600 (subject to weather), free but donations welcome,* which has an interesting exhibition on the death-defying work of lifeboat crews. Up above on West Cliff are elegant houses and Georgian crescents as well as the much-photographed whalebone arch and statue of

Captain Cook. Not far from here, at the **Royal Crescent** on West Cliff, No 6 was the house where Stoker stayed in Whitby (it's marked with a plaque). Down below, heading away from the sea via Baxtergate is the **Station Inn** pub, which once had a river frontage and sat above the entrance to a smuggler's tunnel. Goods were brought into the pub from the river and carried through the tunnel underneath the nearby cottages to a pub where they were distributed. A short distance down Bagdale Street is the impressive Tudor manor house **Bagdale Hall**. Now a hotel and restaurant (see page 65), the building still has many of its original fittings and the massive fireplaces that once provided all the building's heat. Further up Bagdale, behind Broomfield Terrace, is **Victoria Spa**, a circular building with a lantern roof that was popular in the 19th century for its medicinal waters. Nearby, at Pannett Park, is the unique **Whitby Museum** ① *T01947-602908, www.whitbymuseum.org.uk, May-Sep Tue-Sun 0930-1630, £5, under-16s free*, a wonderful, old-fashioned place in which some objects are still explained in script on yellowing notecards. Much of the museum is devoted to the city's heritage among seafarers and whalers. There's still more Cook memorabilia here, including objects his crew brought back from their trips, alongside some unusual fossils – including some from the Jurassic period – that had been discovered in the area.

The **Rail Trail** is a 21-mile traffic-free walking and cycling route following an old railway line from Whitby to Scarborough, with fantastic clifftop views and an impressive railway viaduct just outside of Whitby which crosses over the River Esk. **Trailways** is a bike hire company located on the Rail Trail a few miles out of Whitby; see page 69. Contact the Whitby tourist office, page 52, for more information and a map of the route.

Whitby to Scarborough

Robin Hood's Bay

One of those rare towns that lives up to its fairy tale name, Robin Hood's Bay huddles on the side of sheer cliffs as if it's trying to hide from view. It fails completely, of course, betrayed by its roguish beauty and lovely setting. There's not much in the way of traditional sights here – no museums or castles – but it's just a peaceful and pretty place in which to wander and get lost on its tangled staircases emerging, suddenly, on the windswept headland. Its trademark bright red rooftops seem to stack one on top of each other as the whitewashed stone cottages are built on nearly perpendicular rocks that reach inexorably for the sea. The Bay, as locals call it, does less fishing and more tourism these days, and only a few boats are tied up at the water's edge. The name is one of the many mysteries of the town; nobody knows where it comes from, although legends abound. The least fanciful story is that the Merry Men fled here at some point, and the green one disguised himself as a fisherman until the heat was off.

There's a car park at the top of the hill, and all visitors are required to park there and walk down the steep cobblestone road to the town below; ignore this rule at your peril, as these roads were built for horse-pulled carts, not for Vauxhall Astras. There's one street in the village, its edges sprinkled with a few art shops, souvenir shops and a couple of tiny pubs and restaurants. The rest of the houses are reached by a series of stone staircases. There's no harbour, and houses are built all the way to the water's edge. **The Bay Hotel**, which stands closest to the sea, famously had its windows smashed by the prow of a boat that got too close. The writer Leo Walmsley lived at No 8 King St from 1894 to 1913, and based a series of novels in the fictional fishing village of 'Bramblewick', which acted as a stand-in for Robin Hood's Bay.

Known for its history as a haven for smugglers, it is said that in the 18th century everybody in the town was so complicit in the crimes that goods could be passed from one house to the next, through windows and tunnels, all the way from the harbour to the top of the road. When a cottage on Chapel St was renovated in the 1980s, the owners found a pit under the floorboards big enough to hold four casks of brandy.

You can find out more about smuggling all along the North Yorkshire coast in the national trust centre in the **Old Coastguard Station** ① *The Dock, T01947-885900, www.nationaltrust.org.uk, Mar-Nov daily 1000-1700, rest of the year Sat-Sun 1000-1600, free,* on the edge of the village. There are also interesting exhibits on geology and wildlife in the area.

For sun worshippers, there's a sandy **beach** to one side of the town, and a rocky strip of coast on the other. When the tide is out, this is said to be a good place to find fossils.

Ravenscar

A few miles south of Robin Hood's Bay, some of the best views on the coastline can be had at the ill-fated 'town' of Ravenscar. On red-stone cliffs that soar hundreds of feet above the dark blue sea, the gorgeous view stretches for miles. The area looks like a flat, grassy park, until you study it further and notice that it is arranged like a cul-de-sac. In fact, a developer named John Septimus Bland planned to turn the area into a resort town, and laid out the roads, put in a drainage system and built a couple of shops and houses before realising it was a terrible idea. The perch is too high, the route down to the sea too precarious, and the competition from Whitby and Scarborough too intense for it ever to have worked. He dropped the idea, and the abandoned development now provides handy parking spaces from which to stroll to the isolated **Raven Hall Hotel**, which once acted as George III's hideaway when the mental demons were acting up. The views from the hotel, where the cliffs are up to 250 m high, are extraordinary. Also in Ravenscar is a National Trust **visitor centre** ① *signposted from the A471, T01723-870423, yorkshirecoast@nationaltrust.org.uk, daily late Mar-Oct,* with information on the local area and walks.

Scarborough

Scarborough is one of those towns that looks best from afar: from a distance it glows like a cream-coloured mirage against the backdrop of dark blue sea and green hills. Up close, it's somewhat more tacky, particularly along the waterfront, where casinos, arcades and souvenir shops fight for space with hamburger stands and candy shops. Above it all, the ancient fortifications of Scarborough Castle bristle anachronistically. The castle might be the only attraction here, were it not for a woman named Elizabeth Farrow, who, upon drinking a glass of local spring water in 1620, and noting its mineral taste, pronounced it medicinal. Over the subsequent years, thousands poured into the town to take 'the cure', and the town was built up to cater to them. By the time Queen Victoria took the throne, Scarborough was one of the country's most popular resort towns among the moneyed classes.

Scarborough may once again be undergoing a transformation, albeit on a smaller scale, with its growing surf scene, the opening of new art galleries, the redevelopment of the Rotunda Museum and other development initiatives.

Arriving in Scarborough

Getting there The **train** station is handily located in the centre at the top of the hill on Westborough. **Coaches** and **buses** arrive at the train station. ▸▸ *See Transport, page 69.*

Getting around Scarborough is sprawling, but walkable, if you've got the time. If you prefer to ride, there is a handy park-and-ride bus system that will shuttle you to major sights in town – look for the signs near any of the 12 car parks in the town centre. This is a better option than attempting to drive from one sight to another, as traffic is congested, parking is competitive (lots often fill up early) and the general frustration of trying to find a streetside parking place can take the fun out of the day.

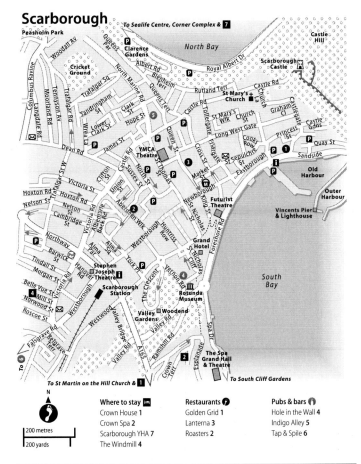

Scarborough

Where to stay 🛏	Restaurants 🍴	Pubs & bars 🍺
Crown House 1	Golden Grid 1	Hole in the Wall 4
Crown Spa 2	Lanterna 3	Indigo Alley 5
Scarborough YHA 7	Roasters 2	Tap & Spile 6
The Windmill 4		

Tourist information There are two TICs in Scarborough. The **Brunswick TIC** ① *Brunswick Shopping Centre, Westborough, T01723-383636, tourismbureau@scarborough. gov.uk, Apr-Jun and Sep-Oct Mon-Sat 0930-1730, Sun 1030-1600, Jul-Aug opens at 0900 on Sat, Nov-Mar Mon-Sat 0930-1700*. There's another office, the **Harbourside** TIC ① *Sandside, contact details as above, Apr-Jun and Sep-Oct 1000-1730, Jul-Aug 0930-1900, Nov-Mar Sat-Sun 1000-1630*, on the South Bay Seafront.

Places in Scarborough

Along the waterfront the amusements are quite obvious. The **North Bay** offers the most places to spend your money with its water slides, games and miniature North Bay Railway. At the far north end, the **Sea Life Centre** ① *T01723-373414, www.visitsealife.com, daily 1000-1600, adults and children £16.20, online £9.72, family per person £13.20/£7.92*, has hands-on aquatic exhibits with aquariums filled with sealife and rockpools. All along the waterfront are carnival rides and games rooms, as well as many opportunities for ocean cruises and speedboat rides. On the curve of the headland, there's nothing but sea views – an acknowledgement of the power of the sea that prevents any development here. The **beach huts** ①*T01723-366102, www.scarboroughbeachhuts.co.uk, £15-25 daily or £60-150 a week, depending on the time of year*, along the front have been freshly painted in bright colours and can be booked for the day or week.

On the other side, the beaches on the **South Bay** are wider and more popular than are those on the north. Here, too, are more silly seaside amusements, but there are also grown-up options in the form of the lush **South Cliff Gardens**, from where there are great views of the town and sea. At one end of the gardens is a funicular railway, the **Spa Cliff Lift** ① *T01723-501754, Feb-Oct daily 0930-1645, 75p*. Also here is the restored **Spa** ① *T01723-357869, www.scarboroughspa.co.uk*, which dates from the 19th century, when the town became a popular spa and a bathing house and assembly rooms were built here. The Spa is now a concert hall and theatre.

From the gardens you can branch out across the cliff-top neighbourhoods to explore the city's lovely Victorian architecture. For fans of Victoriana, the house known as **Woodend** ① *The Crescent, T01723-384500, www.woodendcreative.co.uk, Mon-Fri 0900-1700, free*, is now a contemporary art gallery exhibiting and selling work by local artists. It was once the holiday home of the Sitwell family, famed as writers and philosophers. Of all the buildings in Scarborough, the single most beautiful is the rambling, turreted structure that stands commandingly at the top of the cliff. Still called the **Grand Hotel**, it was a favourite haunt of the rich and famous after its construction in 1867.

Virtually all of the city's museums are at this end of town. The unique round Georgian building on Vernon Road that holds the **Rotunda Museum** ① *T01723-353665, www.rotundamuseum.org.uk, Tue-Sun 1000-1700, £4.50, under-16s free, £5 with entry to Scarborough Art Gallery, see below*, is hard to miss. The best museum in town, the Rotunda holds interesting archaeological remains that have been discovered in the area, including the 3500-year-old body that has come to be known as Gristhorpe Man. He was discovered buried in the trunk of a hollowed oak tree. The museum also has the only information you're likely to find on the Scarborough Fair, which first appeared on the scene when Henry III was king. There's a dinosaur exhibition too, showing fossilized evidence of these creatures in Scarborough.

On Albion Road, the church of **St Martin on the Hill** ⓘ www.st-martin-on-the-hill.org.uk, is home to a collection of pre-Raphaelite art. The pulpit features panels by Rossetti, while other pieces are by Burne-Jones and William Morris. The **Scarborough Art Gallery** ⓘ *The Crescent, T01723-374753, www.rotundamuseum.org.uk, Tue-Sun 1000-1700, £2, under-16s free, £5 with entry to the Rotunda Museum, see above*, is in a handsome Italianate building dating from the 1840s and has permanent and temporary exhibitions.

According to local lore, King Richard III so loved the views from **Scarborough Castle** ⓘ *T01723-372451, www.english-heritage.org.uk, Apr-Sep daily 1000-1800, Oct 1000-1700 daily, Nov-Mar Sat-Sun 1000-1600, £5, under-16s £3, family £13*, that his ghost still returns here today. Richard III had a good eye – the sweeping view from the walls is extraordinary. For nearly 900 years, the castle's rambling ruins have dominated the northern headland, but use of the site as a fortress has been traced back much further than a millennium. Archaeological digs have uncovered items from the Bronze and Iron ages. The Romans used it as a signalling station in the fourth century. The structure that remains dates from 1136, when it was built by William de Gros to replace a wooden fort. Henry II later took the castle for himself – even as he was destroying similar structures around the country as he asserted his authority over the territory – because he saw it as virtually impossible to invade. He was right. Although the castle was repeatedly besieged, it was never taken by force. Still, its isolation was also ultimately its weakness: in 1645 Hugh Chomley's Royalist troops held out for months under attack by John Meldrum's Scottish army, until their food stocks ran out. Even then they fought on until they became too weak to continue. They were allowed to surrender with honour – many of the survivors were so malnourished they had to be carried out of the garrison. Today the barbican, walls and three-storey keep gives an idea of the vastness of the structure that once stood here.

Just down the street from the castle entrance the gothic **St Mary's Church** dates back to 1180, making it nearly as old as the castle that overshadows it. Its shady graveyard contains the tomb of the least known of the Brontë sisters, Anne, who died in Scarborough in 1849.

Scarborough to Hull

Filey

About 8 miles south of Scarborough, Filey is one of the most underrated towns on the coast. This is somewhat understandable, considering that it lacks Scarborough's glitz and Whitby's fame, but with its long expanse of dark sand beach, Edwardian architecture and a general sense of decorum that eludes other seaside towns, Filey has much to offer. Its natural setting, surrounded by dark stone cliffs and green hills, is its primary charm and its **beach** is undeniably the best on the coast, stretching for miles down as far as Flamborough Head to the south. Just north is **Filey Brigg**, with its pleasant nature trails that wander through the hills and down to the shore. For information on **walks** in the area stop in at the **visitor centre** ⓘ *John St, T01723-383636, summer daily 0930-1600, winter daily 0930-1600 (closed 1230-1300) except Wed when it opens at 1000*.

Bempton Cliffs and Flamborough Head

The sheer white cliffs at Bempton, on the B1229 off the A165, plunge hundreds of feet straight down into the chill waters of the North Sea and seem the most inhospitable of places in which to live, but in the summer, thousands of seabirds call them home. The **Bempton Cliffs RSPB nature reserve** ① *T01262-851179, www.rspb.org.uk, visitor centre daily 1000-1700, closing at 1600 Nov-Feb, £5 per car*, was set up to protect the cliffs and to allow safe vantage points for watching the birds in action. From a series of viewing stations along the clifftops you can watch big white gannets wheeling through the skies in search of supper. Between May and early July this is the best place in the country to see impossibly adorable puffins, with their colourful beaks and penguin-like bodies. They nest here in the spring and early summer, but by August their young have grown large enough to head out to their winter grounds. Other birds to be seen include kittiwakes, guillemots and razorbills. Helpful displays help amateurs separate one from another, but binoculars are necessary for a good view. There are RSPB staff to help you identify birds and there is also a visitor centre here. If you're feeling energetic, there's a great 11-mile coastal walk from Bempton Cliffs to Bridlington, following the magnificent chalk cliff.

Just south of Bempton Cliffs, the cliffs at Flamborough Head offer equally spectacular views of chalky white rock and deep blue sea. In 2012 it was named as one of the top 10 places in the UK to spot whales and porpoises. The **Flamborough lighthouse** ① *T01262-673769, www.trinityhouse.co.uk, late Mar to Sep Sat-Thu 1200-1600, Oct Sat-Sun 1200-1600, £3.30, under-16s £2.20*, a mile from the village dates back to the 1700s. Twenty-minute tours operate to the top of the lighthouse or find out more in the visitor centre.

Bridlington

The last of the coastal resort towns in more ways than one, poor Bridlington – or 'Brid' as it's known locally – pales in comparison to its northern neighbours. It's unfair really, considering that the town has stood on this spot for nearly a millennium, but it peaked in the Edwardian years and it's all been downhill ever since, it seems. Today the seafront is its only selling point, particularly its sandy beach and its busy harbour, but Filey's beach is better, and Scarborough's seaside amusements make Bridlington's look tattered. Still, it's less crowded than Scarborough, and, as it specializes in attracting families with children, it offers clean, wholesome fun. There are plenty of amusements and candy shops and little stores with tacky souvenirs.

Hornsea to Spurn Head

Below Bridlington the coastline becomes more empty and forbidding. Hornsea is the last village of any size, and it is known primarily for the eponymous **pottery** that is made here. If you're a fan, there's a factory on the main road, the B1242, which is open for tours and has a good **museum** ① *Burns Farm, 11-17 Newbegin, T01964-533443, www.hornsea museum.com, late Mar to Oct Mon-Sat 1100-1700, Sun 1400-1700, £3, under-16s £2*. The museum consists of an 18th-century farmhouse, with interesting exhibits on rural life from that period, and the pottery, with displays on its history. Near the village is the vast, freshwater **Hornsea Mere**, the largest lake in Yorkshire, and home to flocks of herons. South of Hornsea is mile after mile of empty beach. About 7 miles down the road near Aldbrough is **Burton Constable Hall** ① *T01964-562400, www.burtonconstable.com, Easter-Oct Sat-Thu 1300-1700, grounds and stable from 1100, £6.75, under-16s £3.50, grounds and stable only £3, £1.50*, a manor house that dates back to Elizabethan times. The lovely building – which was altered in the 18th century – has been fitted with period furnishings. Among its 'decorations' are paintings by Renoir, Pissarro and Gainsborough. Its vast grounds were landscaped by Capability Brown.

The end of the Yorkshire coast comes at **Spurn Head** ⓘ *www.ywt.org.uk, visitor centre and café, £3 for cars*, a thin spit of 3.5-mile-long beach that reaches out into the sea, then curves back as if it has changed its mind. It is now a Yorkshire Wildlife Trust nature reserve, and is reached down a toll road from the village of Easington on the B1445. Except for a few animal lovers, you'll often have the whole thing to yourself; well, that is, you and the seals, floating butterflies and seabirds that live protected lives there.

Hull

The area just inland from the south Yorkshire coast is a flat, undistinguished land known as the Wolds. Its miles of farmland are dotted with villages, most of them unspectacular, and there are few features here to convince tourists to take their right foot off the accelerator pedal. In fact Hull itself – which is much better suited to its truncated nickname than by its rarely used full name of Kingston-upon-Hull – is certainly not a tourism hub. It sits at the mouth of the River Humber, an old port city with a reputation as a town of tough guys, and a good place to get beaten up if you stray into the wrong pub at the wrong time. Hull was England's biggest port for centuries, and is still a busy seaport, although these days some of its major docks have been renovated into expensive flats and shining modern shopping malls.

What Hull can offer, however, is a wealth of museums – including the world's only 'submarium' – many of them clustered around its Museum Quarter. Its cultural credentials have received a further boost with the establishment of the Larkin Trail (see page 69), so you can follow in the footsteps of Hull's famous poet.

Arriving in Hull

Getting there The **train** station is on busy Ferensway Street on the west side of town. From the north, the A1079 and the A165 both go to Hull. If you're driving from the west, Hull is on the A63. From the east it's on the A1033. Hull is about 10 miles south of Beverley and 45 miles southeast of York. There is a convenient central **car** park at the Princes Quay shopping centre – it's well signposted. The **bus** station is just to the north of the train station. Ferries from Rotterdam and Zeebrugge arrive at the ferry port on the eastern side of town, and there are shuttlebuses from the dock to the town centre. ▶▶ *See Transport, page 70.*

Getting around Hull is a busy city with a useful bus system. There is a park and ride scheme from Walton Street and Anlaby Road (signposted on main routes into the city) with shuttles every few minutes Monday to Saturday, £1. Otherwise you can catch buses near the train station and the bus station, or from main streets in the city centre. Once you're in the city centre, you can walk to the main sights in the old city and along the waterfront. But a good map is necessary, and the tourist office (see below) can offer guidance and directions to get you started.

Tourist information Hull TIC ⓘ *1 Paragon St, Queen Victoria Sq, T01482-223559, www.hullcc.gov.uk 0900-1800, Mon-Sat 1000-1700, Sun 1100-1500*. You can pick up information and maps are available. See also www.visithullandeastyorkshire.com.

Places in Hull

Princes Quay in particular is the town's main shopping area; a modern shopping mall, it has all the high street shops. Nearby on the waterfront is **The Deep** ① *Tower St, T01482-381000, www.thedeep.co.uk, daily1000-1800, £10.75, children £8.75, families £35,* the city's gleaming aquarium. It's a massive and absorbing place with every imaginable form of sealife.The town's sea-faring history dates back to the 13th century, and you can learn absolutely everything there is to know about that at the **Maritime Museum** ① *T01482-613902, Mon-Sat 1000-1700, Sun 1330-1630, free,* on Queen Victoria Square near the Princes Quay. Appropriately located in the old town Docks Office, the well-designed museum traces the seafaring side of Hull back to the days of Edward I. It also goes into some detail on Hull's whaling history, including hundreds of pieces of (now politically incorrect) whaling technology and memorabilia. There are elaborate whalebone carvings made by sailors, and massive equipment used to handle the giant mammals. It's all quite fascinating if you're not squeamish. Also in Queen Victoria Square is the **Ferens Art Gallery** ① *T01482-300300, www.hullcc.gov.uk, Mon-Sat 1000-1700, Sun 1330-1630, free,* with a good permanent collection and a children's gallery, with art and activities aimed at six- to10-year-olds.

Along with the sea you often get those whose artistic soul is struck by the ocean, and Hull was once home to Philip Larkin, who didn't like it much, and before then the 17th-century poet Andrew Marvell who did. Marvell, like most people who grew up in Hull at the time, attended the Old Grammar School, which now houses the **Hands on History Museum** ① *T01482-300300, www.hullcc.gov.uk, Mon-Sat 1000-1700, Sun 1330-1630, free,* in a 16th-century red-brick building off Trinity House Lane. The school concentrates on historical Hull, and has good interactive exhibits. There is also an Ancient Egypt gallery with an authentic mummy. Not far from the school is the city's traditional market area, with its indoor **market hall** ① *0730-1700 Mon-Sat,* and on Tuesdays, Fridays and Saturdays a colourful outdoor market is open adjacent to the indoor version. Not far from the markets down Trinity House Lane the handsome **Holy Trinity Church** makes for a pretty picture, and a few blocks past the Hands on History Museum is the small, cobblestone area that makes up old Hull. While there's not much to it (German bombs destroyed much of historic Hull during the Second World War), you can peek in at the wrought-iron staircase and ornate stucco work of the **Maister House** ① *160 High St, T01723-879900, www.nationaltrust.org.uk, Mon-Fri 1000-1600, only hall and staircase open for viewing,* a restored, 18th-century home.

Further along is the so-called Museums Quarter, a collection of four museums run by Hull City Council located on or near the High Street. **Wilberforce House** ① *23-25 High St, T01482-300300, www.hullcc.gov.uk, Mon-Sat 1000-1700, Sun 1330-1630, free,* is the former home of William Wilberforce, who was the leading campaigner for abolition of slavery in the British Empire. The Jacobean house is now a monument to the anti-slavery movement and includes a small but interesting collection of memorabilia and information on Wilberforce's work. There is also an exhibition on West African culture. Behind the house on the waterfront you can climb onto a restored fishing boat, the **Arctic Corsair** ① *T01482-300300, www.hullcc.gov.uk, late Mar-Oct Wed and Sat 1000-1630, Sun 1330-1630, entry by free guided tour only,* to give you an idea of what it was like for those who lived and worked on the sea. Near the *Arctic Corsair* is the **Streetlife Museum of Transport** ① *High St, T01482-300300, www.hullcc.gov.uk, Mon-Sat 1000-1700, Sun 1330-1630, free,* with exhibits on trains, cars, horse carriages and bikes, as well as a replica of a historic street in Hull. Also on High Street is the **Hull and East Riding Museum** ① *36 High St, T01482-300300, www.hullcc.gov.uk, Mon-Sat 1000-1700, Sun 1330-1630, free*, where you can explore the region's archaeology and geology dating from paleolithic times. Exhibits include a woolly mammoth, a replica Iron Age settlement and a Viking sword.

Beverley

It's easy to see that this bustling, mid-sized town 10 miles north of Hull was once a market centre for the region, and though the streets have been widened and the old shopfronts replaced with modern high street façades, you can still see how the streets once curved around to a broad open-air market.

Arriving in Beverley
Getting there The train station is near Station Square near the Minster, and coaches stop just around the corner in the square.

Tourist information **Beverley TIC** ① *34 Butcher Row, T01482-391672, beverleytic@east riding.gov.uk, Mon-Fri 0930-1715, Sat 1000-1645, Jul-Aug Sun 1100-1500.*

Places in Beverley
Today, aside from the interesting layout of the town, and the lovely minster, Beverley manages not to feel historic; quite a feat for a town in which 350 buildings are listed. This town, the childhood home of Mary Wollstonecraft (1759-97), still feels like a modern town, and so things like the old **North Bar** – the only of the city's medieval gates still standing – come as something of a surprise. While not as elaborate as York's gates, the gate at the busy corner of Hengate and North Bar, is quite pretty, and gives you some idea of how very much the town has changed since its 14th-century construction. Heading down North Bar toward the centre, the church of **St Mary's** ① *T01482-869137, stmarysbeverley.org*, the lesser of the town's two churches, is small but exquisitely detailed. Because it has been altered repeatedly over the years, it is hard to date it by just looking at it, but its oldest section – the south porch – dates back to the 14th century, while most of it was built before the 15th century. Inside you may quickly develop a pain in your neck from staring up at its painted ceilings, with portraits of every king from Sigebert to Henry VI. Everywhere are wall carvings, most with a musical theme. The town was known for its minstrels, whose work provided much of the financing for the decoration inside the church – thus there are carvings of lutes, horns and drums. Finding the cute little 'Pilgrim's Rabbit' carving (we'll not give away its hiding place) is part of the fun of coming here.

Most people who come to Beverley are drawn by its **Minster** ① *beverleyminster.org.uk, Mon-Sat Mar-Oct 0900-1700, May-Aug open until 1730, Nov-Feb 0900-1600, Sun 1200-1730, donation requested, ground floor tours £5, roof tours £5, ground floor and roof tour £7, under-16s £2.50, £2.50 and £3.50*, which is on the other side of the town centre from **St Mary's**. You can't really miss it, as its twin towers are the tallest structures in the town. Once a humble chapel, it became a monastery in the eighth century, under the leadership of a monk called John of Beverley. His body still lies under the nave, and after he was canonized, pilgrims made regular journeys to the church to worship and to donate money. Kings from Athelstan to Henry V credited their pilgrimages here with victories in battle, and so they showered the church with gifts. All of this funded constant expansions until the church grew to its current jaw-dropping size. The west front, which dates from the early 15th century, is considered by many to be the most beautiful part of the building. Inside, the Saxon sanctuary chair was built in the 10th century. The 16th-century oak choir is one of the most perfectly preserved in the country. The Percy Tomb on the north side of the altar – believed to be the tomb of Lady Idoine Percy (who died in 1365) – is a masterpiece of medieval art.

Behind the minster, on Friars Lane, are a few buildings that were once part of the Dominican friary founded in 1240. The Beverley friary is namedropped by Chaucer in his *Canterbury Tales*.

Coastal Yorkshire listings

Staithes p50

Most accommodation in town is in B&Bs, although several of the restaurants and pubs also rent out rooms.

££ Roraima House, 40 Staithes La, T01947-841423, www.bedand breakfast-staithes.co.uk. Lovely Victorian house once owned by the captain of SS Roraima, with sea views from its rooms. Wi-Fi and parking available.

Whitby p51

Most accommodation in Whitby is in guesthouses and B&Bs, although there are a few small hotels. B&Bs are clustered on the West Cliff.

££££-£££ Bagdale Hall Hotel, 1 Bagdale St, T01947-602958, www.bagdale.co.uk. A beautiful Tudor mansion, Bagdale has some rooms with 4-poster beds, and a good restaurant (see Restaurants below). 3-course breakfast and parking included.

£££ Cliffemount Hotel, Runswick Bay, T01947-840103, www.cliffemount hotel.co.uk. This 1920s hotel perches on the cliff above town, 5 miles from Whitby, and offers panoramic views of the countryside. Many rooms have sea views.

£££ La Rosa Hotel, T01947-606981, larosa.co.uk. Unique and fun hotel decorated in a boudoir-kitsch style in a building where Lewis Carroll used to stay. Aptly enough, you can hire the tea room for your very own Mad Hatter's tea party. The emphasis is firmly on vintage,with brass beds, antique accessories and velvet curtains.

£££ Saxonville Hotel, Ladysmith Av, T01947-602631, www.saxonville.co.uk. On the West Cliff overlooking the town, Saxonville has well-appointed rooms.

£££ The White House Hotel, Upgang La, T01947-600469, www.white house-whitby.co.uk. A favourite with golfers, this 2-star hotel overlooks Whitby Golf Course and Sandsend Bay.

£££ The Woodlands, The Valley, Sandsend, T01947-893438, www.thewoodlands-sands end.com. Beautifully renovated intimate hotel set in a peaceful, secluded valley near the beach, a few miles north of Whitby. The 5 rooms are stylishly decorated and there's a superb café/restaurant a few mins' walk away (see Restaurants below). It's very popular, so book well in advance.

££ Union Place, 9 Upgang La, T01947-605501, www.unionplace whitby.co.uk. This small but perfectly formed Georgian B&B offers just 2 rooms in a lovely building 5 mins' walk from the town centre. Parking.

£ Whitby YHA, East Cliff, T0845-371 9049, www.yha.org.uk. This excellent hostel has a spectacular location beside the abbey at the top of East Cliff overlooking Whitby, the sea and the moors. Most beds in dorms. Limited parking. Free entry to Whitby Abbey.

Robin Hood's Bay p55

There are many B&Bs here, but the most desirable accommodation are the self-catering cottages; get a list from the tourist office in Whitby (see page 52) or see www.robin-hoods-bay.co.uk.

£££ Victoria Hotel, at the top of the hill, T01947-880205, www.victoriarhb.com. A grand Victorian structure with sweeping views of the sea, and a popular bar.

£££-££ Thorpe Hall, Middlewood La, Fylingthorpe, T01947-880667, www.thorpe-hall.co.uk. Elizabethan manor house set in lovely grounds a short walk from Robin Hood's Bay.

££ Boathouse Rooms, at the foot of the cliff, T01947-880099, www.boathouserhb.co.uk. 5 comfortable, cosy rooms, as well as the pretty but tiny self-catering **Boathouse Apartment** for 2 people (minimum stay 2 nights).

£ Boggle Hole YHA, Mill Beck, Fylingthorpe, T0845-371 9504, www.yha.org. Set in a narrow valley just metres from the cliffs and the coastal path in a former corn mill. It's a short walk to Robin Hood's Bay, a mile away.

Scarborough *p56, map p57*

Most restaurants are atop the north and south cliffs, and there are quite a few B&Bs clustered in the area around the train station.

£££ Crown House, 20 Filey Rd, T01723-375401, www.crownhouse scarborough.co.uk. Smart B&B with 2 rooms in a handsome Victorian house 20 mins' walk from the centre and 5 mins from the Esplanade. They serve great breakfasts too. It's also available as a self-catering option.

£££ Crown Spa Hotel, The Esplanade, T01723-357400, www.crownspahotel.com. The most elegant hotel in Scarborough, this is a lovely 19th-century building with excellent views, outstanding facilities including a health club and spa and a fabulous indoor pool surrounded by statues.

£££ The Windmill, Mill St, off Victoria Rd, T01723-372735, www.scarborough-windmill-hotel.co.uk. Surely the most unique place to stay in town, this B&B offers, as the name implies, rooms and apartments inside an 18th-century windmill near the centre of Scarborough. Book the balcony room to panoramic views.

£££ Wrea Head Hall, Barmoor La, Scalby, just outside Scarborough, T01723-371190, www.wreaheadhall.co.uk. A stunning place offering peace and beauty on over 4 ha of secluded woodlands.

££ Holly Croft, 28 Station Rd, Scalby, T01723-375376, www.holly-croft.co.uk. Comfortable B&B 3 miles from Scarborough and a mile from the Cleveland Way.

££ Scarborough YHA, Burniston Rd, Scalby Mills, T0845-371 9657. Located in a picturesque old watermill outside the town centre on the A165 and conveniently perched

at the edge of the popular Cleveland Way. It's only 15 mins' walk to the sea.

Hull *p61*

As this isn't a tourism hub, it's fairly easy to find a room here, whether you've booked or not. But most are personality-free chain hotels.

£££-££ Holiday Inn Hull Marina, Castle St, T0871-423 4942, www.hihull marinahotel.co.uk. One of the best hotels in the city, with a view of the river.

££ Mercure Hull Royal, 170 Ferensway, T01482-325087, www.hotels-hull.co.uk. Chain hotel but handily located next to the station. The Old Grey Mare, T01482-448193, goodnightinns.co.uk. Opposite the university.

££ Old Grey Mare, Cottingham Rd, T01482-448193, www.flaminggrillpubs.com. Good-value rooms in this pub opposite the university.

£ Paull Holme Farm, Thorngumbald Rd, Paull, T01964-625893. Fantastic value rooms in this B&B on a farm next to a nature reserve 6 miles east of Hull. Breakfast included.

Beverley *p63*

£££-££ White's Overnight, 12a North Bar Without, T01482-866121, www.whites restaurant.co.uk. Four comfortable rooms offered above a superb restaurant (see below). Good offers on rooms and dining.

££ Beverley Arms Hotel, North Bar Within, T01482-869241, thebeverleyarms.co.uk. Offers historic luxury with some rooms overlooking St Mary's Church. Free Wi-Fi.

££-£ YHA Beverley Friary, Friars La, T0845-371 9004, www.yha.org.uk. This hostel has the best setting in town, in a 13th-century Dominican friary opposite the Minster.

🍴 Restaurants

Whitby *p51*

There are only a few decent restaurants here.

£££-££ Estbek House, East Row, Sandsend, T01947-893424, www.estbekhouse.co.uk. Award-winning restaurant just outside of

Whitby in a Georgian building. Delicious locally caught seafood. Also has rooms (**££**).

££ Bagdale Hall, see Where to stay. Offers excellent traditional European cuisine in a gorgeous historic setting at surprisingly reasonable prices.

££ Green's, 13 Bridge St, T01947-600284, www.greensof whitby.com. The kitchen at this award-winning bistro and restaurant offers creative modern cuisine using local fish and game. Booking is essential at weekends.

££ Harry's Lounge Bar & Brasserie, T01947-601909, www.harrysloungebar.co.uk. Smart central bar serving champagne and cocktails, alongside tapas, with a restaurant upstairs overlooking the port featuring freshly caught seafood and locally sourced meat on the menu. Also has rooms (**££**) with great views, the best of which is the suite.

££ The Woodland Eat, Sandsend, T01947-893438, www.thewoodlands-sandsend.com. Small, quirky café on the seafront at Sandsend owned by **The Woodlands** (see Where to stay), with chalkboard menus and tables outside.

££-£ Magpie Café, 14 Pier Rd, T01947-602058, www.magpiecafe.co.uk. This has to be one of the world's largest fish and chips shops, described by Rick Stein as the best in Britain. It's also a long-established Whitby institution and not to be missed. But the queues are enormous in the high season, so be prepared to wait.

Robin Hood's Bay *p55*

There's not much choice in this tiny village, but you can still get a good pint of ale and a hearty meal.

££ Bramblewick. Once the village bakery, this characterful 17th-century building now houses a restaurant-café with great food using Yorkshire ingredients. Also has 4 rooms (**££**).

£ Swell, Chapel St, T01947-880180, www.swellcafe.co.uk. In an 18th-century former chapel is this funky café, bar and cinema (using pews as seating) rolled into

one, also exhibiting artwork. Soak up the stupendous views of the sea and the village from the café terrace.

Scarborough *p56, map p57*

Most dining options in Scarborough are of the lowest common denominator variety: cheap seafront chippies, tattered cafés and pizza places abound.

£££-££ Lanterna, 33 Queen St, T01723-3636161, www.lanterna-ristorante.co.uk. This fabulous restaurant is renowned for its excellent Italian cuisine, cooked by chef Giorgio who insists on using locally sourced fish, meat and fresh produce and makes the pasta himself. Recommended.

£ Golden Grid Waterside, 4 Sandside, T01723-360922, www.goldengrid.co.uk. Said to offer the best fish and chips in town, established in 1883 and still going strong.

Cafés

Roasters, Aberdeen Walk, T07971-808549, www.roasterscoffee.co.uk. Wide range of coffees, as well as sandwiches and salads. One of several smart coffee places in town.

Bridlington *p60*

£ Little Organic Bakery, 12 Wellington Rd, T07853-303049. Fabulous vegetarian and vegan fare, including great homemade cakes.

Hull *p61*

££ 1884 Dock Street Kitchen, Humber Dock St, T01482-222260, www.1884dockstreet kitchen.co.uk. New swanky addition to Hull's marina in a former shipping building, this large restaurant offers good British cuisine, a great selection of wine and an excellent value 'market menu' for set lunches and dinners.

££ Cerutti's, 10 Nelson St, T01482-328501, www.cerutti.co.uk. Hull's best-known restaurant offers excellent seafood at relatively reasonable prices near the waterfront.

££ Lucca Bar & Kitchen, 84 Princes Av, T01482-470088, wwwluccahull.co.uk. Popular cocktail bar and Italian restaurant serving well-prepared food in a friendly atmosphere.
££-£ Hitchcock's, 1 Bishop La, T01482-320233, www.hitchcocks restaurant.co.uk. Lots of character, this vegetarian restaurant serves buffet meals only, with the first group to book choosing the cuisine of a country, from Indian to Italian.

Beverley *p63*
££ Cerutti's 2, Station Sq, T01482-866700, www.ceruttis.co.uk. Located in the former railway waiting rooms, this is a sister to the restaurant of the same name in Hull and offers similar seafood dishes in rich sauces.
££ Pipe and Glass Inn, West End, South Dalton, T01430-810246, www.pipeand glass.co.uk. An award-winning pub with a Michelin-starred restaurant, this place still manages to retain an unpretentious feel. You can also stay in one of their beautifully designed rooms (**££££-£££**)
££ White's, see Where to stay. Small, smart restaurant serving top-notch lunches and dinners.

🎵 Pubs, bars and clubs

Whitby *p51*
The best pubs in town are on Church St on the east bank of the river.
Duke of York, T01947-600324, at the bottom of the 199 steps, www.dukeofyork.co.uk. Popular pub with great views and good food.
Station Inn, New Quay Rd, T01947-603937, www.stationinn whitby.co.uk. Friendly pub with a good choice of real ales and live music Fri-Sun evenings.

Robin Hood's Bay *p55*
Ye Dolphin, King St, T01947-880337. Tiny fishermen's pub which can get wonderfully raucous on weekend nights.

Scarborough *p56, map p57*
Hole in the Wall, Vernon Rd. A small pub with an excellent selection of ale and regular live music.
Indigo Alley, 4 North Marine Rd, T01723-350599, www.facebook.com/indigoalley. Friendly pub with live music Fri and Sat nights and real ale.
Tap and Spile, 94 Falsgrave Rd, T01723-363837. Real ale pub with live music on Sun. Also does Sun lunch.

Hull *p61*
Ye Olde White Hart, 25 Silver St, www.yeoldewhitehart. Atmospheric 16th-century pub with a remarkable history; a skull was discovered here and Hull's leaders played their part in the Civil War in the pub's Plotter's Room.

Beverley *p63*
White Horse Inn, 22 Hengate, www.nellies.co.uk. Near St Mary's is this pub, known locally as Nellies, with old-fashioned original decor complete with gaslights.

🎭 Entertainment

Scarborough *p56, map p57*
Theatres and live music
Scarborough's summer theatre scene has been renowned for years.
Futurist Theatre, Foreshore Rd, T01723-365789, www.futuristtheatre.co.uk. Theatre staging musicals, concerts and other shows. Also a cinema.
Open-air Theatre, T0844-844 0444, www.scarboroughopenairtheatre.com. Originally home of *It's a Knockout* In the 1960s, this is now one of North Yorkshire's biggest music venues. It reopened in 2010 after a multi-million pound makeover and has already attracted names such as Elton John.
Spa, see page 58. The revamped Spa hosts concerts, orchestra performance and musicals.
Stephen Joseph Theatre, Westborough, T01723-370541, www.sjt.uk.com. High quality

performances – often with casts from London theatre – is to be had at the theatre, where most of the plays premier of Sir Alan Ayckbourn, the former artistic director. The theatre also screens films and has a good restaurant.

Hull *p61*
Hull Truck Theatre Company,
50 Ferensway, www.hulltuck.co.uk. Brilliant theatre where performances are often ground breaking.

⚙ Festivals

Whitby *p51*
Last weekend Apr and first weekend of Nov Goth Weekend. If you feel besieged by Marilyn Manson lookalikes in Whitby, it might be because Goths hit the town a couple of times each year for this major festival to parade their black lipstick and pay homage to Bram Stoker. See also www.whitbygothweekend.co.uk.
Aug Regatta. Features beautiful boats and a fireworks show over the harbour. The Whitby Challenge Cup takes place at the same time. See www.whitbyregatta.co.uk.
Aug Whitby Folk Week. When the town fills with singers, bands, dancers, storytellers and artists, and music can be heard on every street corner. See www.whitbyfolk.co.uk.

Scarborough *p56, map p57*
Jul Seafest, a 3-day maritime festival on the harbour. See www.scarboroughseafest.com.
Sep Scarborough Jazz Festival, one of the top jazz festivals in the UK, on 27-29 Sep in 2013. See www.scarboroughjazzfestival.co.uk.

Hull *p61*
Sep Freedom Festival celebrates arts and music. See www.freedomfestival.co.uk.
Oct Hull Fair. The most popular local event is a massive affair that fills the town with carnival rides and candyfloss for a solid week in early Oct.

⚠ What to do

Whitby *p51*
Cycle hire
Trailways, Hawkser Station, T01947-820207, www.trailways.info. Bike hire on the Rail Trail Whitby–Scarborough cycle route. Prices at around £25 a day; 2 hr rates available in school holidays.

Hull *p61*
Walking
Larkin Trail, www.thelarkintrail.co.uk. This walk links 25 locations that are important in the work of Hull's best-known modern poet, Philip Larkin.

◉ Transport

Whitby *p51*
Bus
Yorkshire Coastliner, T01653-692556, www.yorkbus.co.uk, services connect **Leeds** and **York** with the coast. **National Express**, T08717-818178, www.nationalexpress.com, buses to **London** (8 hrs 10 mins).

Train
Trains run 4 times daily to **Middlesbrough** (1 hr 30 mins). Getting to **London King's Cross** involves 2 changes, at York and Middlesbrough (4 hrs 50 mins). The North York Moors Railway operates a service to **Pickering** and stations en route in the North York Moors National Park; see page 44.

Scarborough *p56, map p57*
Trains leave regularly for **Hull** (1 hr 30 mins), **Leeds** (1 hr 15 mins) and **York** (50 mins). For **London King's Cross** (3 hrs) change in York.

Scarborough to Hull *p59*
Train and bus
Trains run from Filey to **Bridlington**, **Hull** and **Scarborough**. There's also an hourly bus service connecting Filey with Bridlington and Scarborough.

Hull *p61*
Bus
Hull is served by **National Express**,
T08717-818178, www.nationalexpress.com,
buses to **London** (7 hrs).

Train
There are regular trains to **Leeds** (1 hr),
London King's Cross (2 hrs 30 mins, with
services hourly), **Scarborough** (1 hr 30 mins)
and **York** (1 hr).

Hull *p61*
Medical facilities Hull Royal Infirmary,
Anlaby Rd, T01482-875875.

Contents

South & West Yorkshire

South Yorkshire is marked by miles of rolling green hills, with rich farmland and horse pastures. The old steel town of Sheffield is the fitting centre of this region, with its steep hilly streets, old millstreams and wonderfully gloomy architecture. At the edge of the Pennines and the Yorkshire Dales, West Yorkshire is a hilly evocative country where miles of farmland are interrupted by the busy college town of Leeds, with its non-stop nightlife and funky, laid-back atmosphere. This is where Brontë country begins, the area that inspired the dark Gothic tales that have led generations to wonder just what is so romantic about the heather on the hill. Thousands of tourists each year descend upon the town of Haworth seeking more understanding of the famous family and its doomed daughters. The old spa town of Harrogate has hardly changed at all in the last century, except to change the signs from welcoming the upper class to welcoming the business class.

Sheffield → *For listings, see pages 86-92.*

The unofficial capital of South Yorkshire, Sheffield went from feast to famine over the course of a century or so. Once the affluent industrial centre of the country, its modern, and largely unattractive appearance is a result of the fact that it was nearly obliterated by German bombs during the Second World War. Reconstruction after the war was hurried and paid little attention to aesthetics, and the city developed a sterile and ugly appearance, so much so that it acquired the local motto of 'the city that Hitler built on his way home'. Still, it has some remnants of its old beauty, in dark, red-brick Victorian buildings that dot its hilly streets.

The city had just finished rebuilding when the steel industry that had made it such a target in the first place, shifted from the developed to the developing world. After that, Sheffield lost its point. Thousands of jobs disappeared in the 1970s and 80s, and the city became synonymous with poverty. To claw its way out of recession, Sheffield diversified its business base and embraced tourism and the arts. These days it is a city in transition, with a vibrant nightlife and music scene and a burgeoning arts movement. Its attempts to expand its economy have not been as successful, though, and it still struggles to reach financial stability. Its biggest attractions are its modern museums and the grand buildings that survived the war.

Arriving in Sheffield
Getting there Sheffield's **train** station is about 15 minutes' walk east of the centre of town near Sheaf Square. Sheffield is on the A57 from the east or west and on the A629 from the north, and the A61 from the south. The Sheffield Interchange bus station is on Pond St. ▸▸ *See Transport, page 91.*

Getting around Sheffield is a big, bustling city, and walking is generally not an option, particularly because many of its museums are on the outskirts of the city. You can walk around the city centre, however, and a good place to start is at the tourist office at the Winter Garden (see below). Local public transport includes numerous buses and the handy **Supertram** ① *T0114-272 8282, www.supertram.com*. Most buses depart from the High Street. Fare and timetable information are available at a **Travel Information Centre** ① interchange, Pond Sq, Mon-Fri 0800-1800, Sat 0900-1700, or at Arundel Gate, Mon-Fri 0700-1800, Sat 0900-1700. Alternatively, you can contact **Traveline** ① *T01709-515151*.

Tourist information Sheffield TIC ① *Winter Garden, Surrey St, T0114-221 1900, visitor@marketingsheffield.org, Mon-Fri 0930- 1700, Sat 0930-1600, closed 1300-1330*. It can, and will, bury you in maps, brochures and guides, and can book accommodation. See also www.welcometosheffield.co.uk.

Places in Sheffield

Winning the gold star for 'most improved part of Sheffield' – and the obvious place to start any tour – is the **Cultural Industries Quarter**. This is a renovated section of town near the train station filled with hip nightclubs and art galleries, as well as offices. One of the best of the galleries in this area is the contemporary art centre, the **Site Gallery** ① *Brown St, T0114 281 2077, www.sitegallery.org, Tue-Sat 1100-1730, free*, with its acclaimed collection of photography and multimedia work. More art collections worth your attention can be found in the centre of town. The **Graves Art Gallery** ① *T0114-278 2600, www.museums-sheffield.org.uk, Wed-Fri 1000-1500 Sat 1100-1500, free*, is on the top floor of the Central Library. It has a surprisingly solid collection of works by European artists including pieces by Matisse, Turner and Nash, as well as more recent names such as Damien Hirst, Marc Quinn and Bridget Riley, in a modern setting. Near Graves Art Gallery is the **Millennium Gallery** ① *Arundel Gate, T0114-278 2600, www.museums-sheffield.org.uk, Mon-Sat 1000-1700, Sun 1100-1600, free*, showing work by local artists, Ruskin, crafts, metalwork and temporary exhibitions from galleries such as the Tate.

The library is located near the Gothic-Victorian **Town Hall** on Pinstone Street, which gets its distinctive dark look from the Derbyshire stone from which it is made. The green space in front of the town hall is the **Peace Garden**, with its fountains and summertime flowers. Another green space near the Peace Garden is the impressive **Winter Garden** ① *Mon-Sat 0800-2000, Sun 0800-1800, free*, a huge greenhouse 70 m long and 22 m high, home to a vast array of plants from around the world.

If you head south down Division Street from the town centre you enter the vibrant **Devonshire Quarter,** which is the hippest shopping section of Sheffield, with many independent shops and bars. This is where the students from Sheffield University stock up on their vintage clothes and CDs. There's a café culture here that you won't find elsewhere in town, and it's a great place to sit outside and sip a cappuccino, while looking as cool as possible.

If you head north from the town centre, the area around the medieval **Church of St Peter and St Paul** marks the centre of old Sheffield. Although much altered over the years, the church dates back to the 15th century. Its Lady Chapel contains the tomb of the sixth Earl of Shrewsbury, who served as the keeper of Mary, Queen of Scots, when she was imprisoned in Sheffield from 1570-84. If you head east on Church Street from here, you reach **Castle Market**,

Sheffield

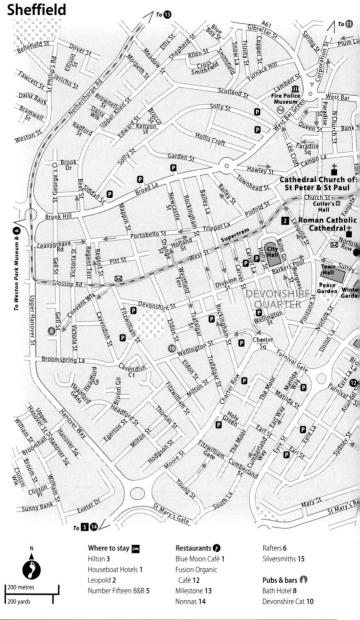

N

200 metres
200 yards

Where to stay 🛏
Hilton **3**
Houseboat Hotels **1**
Leopold **2**
Number Fifteen B&B **5**

Restaurants 🍴
Blue Moon Café **1**
Fusion Organic
 Café **12**
Milestone **13**
Nonnas **14**

Rafters **6**
Silversmiths **15**

Pubs & bars 🍸
Bath Hotel **8**
Devonshire Cat **10**

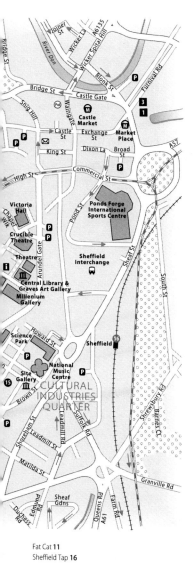

Fat Cat **11**
Sheffield Tap **16**

the city's largest indoor market, and the very scant remains of **Sheffield Castle**, where she was held. There is next to nothing to see here, though, as the ruins are all but gone. Across from the church is the old **Cutler's Hall** ① *T0114-2728456, www.cutlershall.co.uk, occasionally open to the public.* Sheffield was once the centre of the cutlery industry, and this 1832 building was their headquarters. It is much more fabulous on the inside than on the outside, and there is an extraordinary collection of silver here, but it's a private events venue so isn't usually open to the public.

There are yet more art museums to the west of the town centre. The refurbished **Weston Park Museum** ① *T0114-278 2600, www.museums-sheffield.org.uk, Mon-Fri 1000-1600, Sat 1000-1700, Sun 1100-1600, free, Nos 51 and 52 buses or take the tram to the University of Sheffield and walk 650 m,* is in a neoclassical building in Weston Park, and houses much of the city's art collection that is not in the Graves Gallery, as well as housing the city museum's main collections, with more cutlery and locally made art and objects, including lots of interactive ones and Snowy the (stuffed) polar bear.

Better than these, for those really interested in Sheffield, is the excellent **Kelham Island Museum** ① *Alma St, off Corporation St, T0114-272 2106, www.simt. co.uk, Mon-Thu 1000-1600, Sun 1100-1645, £4.50, under-16s free,* a mile north of the city centre on Kelham Island, where vast exhibitions display objects that tell the story of Sheffield's industrial past. There's a 12,000 horsepower steam engine that is started up every day, and a steel gallery tells the story of the city's steelmaking history. Children can even get processed like steel in the Melting Shop. A transport gallery has some Sheffield- produced vehicles from the 1920s.

Kids can get further hands-on experiences at **Magna** ① *Sheffield Rd, Rotherham, T01709-720002, www.visitmagna.co.uk, daily 1000-1700, online £9.85, under-16s £8.05, 10% more at Magna on the day, well signposted off the M1*, located on a huge former steelworks site. At this science adventure centre little ones can get up to their knees in industrial equipment, musical devices and more. This place is so innovative and advanced that it is one of the most popular attractions in the area. There's also a large outdoor playground and, from Easter to October, a wet play area.

Leeds and around

The cultural centre of Yorkshire, Leeds is still living down a reputation as a northern industrial town. For years that reputation was deserved, but much has changed. Over the last few decades central Leeds has been refurbished and its grand Victorian buildings restored. Industrial sections have been converted into posh modern shopping and residential arcades. Everywhere there are cafés with outdoor tables (in defiance of the weather), cool, modern bars and upscale department stores. The presence of thousands of university students adds a constant infusion of youth – along with crowded nightclubs, excellent music shops and cheap second-hand clothes shops – while the many museums, the West Yorkshire Playhouse and Opera North provide an acclaimed art sector.

Arriving in Leeds
Getting there Leeds/Bradford International Airport ① *T0871-288 2288, www.leeds bradfordairport.co.uk*, is approximately 10 miles northwest of Leeds City centre and has a variety of links by train (services every 30 minutes), bus (every 30 minutes with Airport Direct buses, T0113-245 7676, www.wymetro.com) and road (clearly signposted from the M1, M62 and A1). The impressively big and busy Leeds City **train** station is in the town centre in front of City Square. The **bus** and **coach** station is nearby on St Peter's Street behind Kirkgate Market. Local buses also set out from here, as well as from stops throughout Leeds. ▸▸ *See Transport, page 91.*

Getting around Leeds has an extensive **bus** system, but most of the sights are in the compact city centre, and few visitors ever need the buses, unless they're going to the few far-flung sights. The **train** station makes an easy starting point for a walking tour, but buses can be caught on St Peter Street, a short walk from the train station. The tourist office (see below) has helpful maps and information about transport. Taxis are plentiful and affordable, and there's a rank adjacent to the train station.

Tourist information Leeds TIC ① *The Arcade, inside the train station, T0113-242 5242, www.visitleeds.co.uk, Mon 1000-1730, Tue-Sat 0900-1730, Sun 1000-1600*, is a large and helpful tourist office which can weigh you down with free maps, guides and advice.

Central Leeds
The area around the train station provides the best examples of Leeds' massive Victorian architecture. From the second you step out of the station you are surrounded by the statues and overly elaborate bronze gas lamps that the Victorians so loved. The area directly in front of the station is the pedestrianized **City Square**, at an intersection of several busy streets,

with cafés and 19th-century statues including the Black Prince on horseback and Joseph Priestley, James Watt, John Harrison and Dean Hook. The Gothic church on the east side of the square is the **Mill Hill Chapel** where Priestley was minister in the mid-1700s.

The obvious next stop on any wander around central Leeds is down Park Row, past a row of well-restored 19th-century office buildings then continuing up The Headrow to the domineering **Leeds Town Hall**, just a few blocks away. The enormous 19th-century building has every imaginable decoration: stone lions, a clocktower, sculptures and columns. Architect Cuthbert Brodrick used everything in his bag of architectural tricks on this one. Next door to the Town Hall, the **Leeds Art Gallery** ① *T0113-247 8256, www.leeds.gov.uk, Mon-Sat 1000-1700 (Wed open from 1200), Sun 1300-1700, free*, houses one of the biggest and best modern art collections in the north of England. It has a clear British emphasis with a constantly changing display of selections from its vast permanent collection of mostly 19th- and 20th-century art including works by Courbet, Sisley, Constable and Crome. Particularly notable is its collection of works by Henry Moore (who studied at the Leeds School of Art). Contemporary art includes works by Paula Rego, Bridget Riley, Mark Wallinger and Alison Wilding. The adjacent **Henry Moore Institute** ① *www.henry-moore.org, Tue-Sun 1100-1730, Wed until 2000, free*, features more works and information on the sculptor and changing exhibitions of sculptures by other artists. The institute also features a study of the art of sculpture and a library.

A few minutes' walk behind the Town Hall is **Leeds City Museum** ① *Millennium Square, T0113-224 3732, www.leeds.gov.uk, Tue-Fri and bank holiday Mon 1000-1700, open until 1900 on Wed, Sat-Sun 1100-1700, free*, is a great introduction to the city, with a large map of Leeds on the floor in the main hall and displays and films on Leeds' history and its communities. There are also exhibitions on natural history, archaeology and world cultures.

East of here, **Briggate** is a pedestrianized lane of shops and businesses in 19th-century buildings with all the filigree, stained glass and marble you could dream of. This section of town has been elegantly restored, and best of all is the frilly arcade of the **Victoria Quarter** where **Harvey Nichols** has planted its northern flag – along with other expensive shops – to the eternal joy of local ladies who lunch. While its clothes are a draw, as in London, its posh café is the biggest attraction for many. Also on Briggate, **St John's Church** is a lovely, Gothic structure built in 1632. Its screen, pews and pulpit are all original. In spring 2013 a spanking new huge shopping centre opened here, called **Trinity Leeds**, from Briggate to Albion Street to Commercial Street. It features a food court and Everyman cinema (see page 90).

More shopping calls for your attention from **Kirkgate Market** ① *www.leedsmarkets.co.uk, daily 0800-1730*, across Vicar Lane from Harvey Nics. Marketers have been peddling wares here since medieval times. The market is the largest in Yorkshire and is set up in a lovely Edwardian building. An outdoor market hosts second-hand clothes stalls every Monday, an Asian Bazaar on Wednesday and a flea market every Thursday. Beyond Vicar Lane, Eastgate continues to Quarry Hill to the acclaimed **West Yorkshire Playhouse**, see page 90.

Follow Vicar Lane down to Duncan Street to reach the **Corn Exchange** ① *Call La, T0113-234 0363, www.leedscornexchange.co.uk, Mon-Sat 1000-1800, Thu until 1900, Sun 1030-1630*, a covered market in a beautifully restored oval Victorian building. This market is decidedly more upscale than Kirkgate with its boutique independent shops selling hand-made jewellery, gifts and vintage clothes. Just behind the exchange is one of Leeds' most fashionable neighbourhoods. The **Exchange Quarter** is filled with cool cafés, upscale restaurants, arty stores and hip bars.

On the water

The once grim industrial section of Leeds along the Leeds–Liverpool Canal was a symbol for urban blight. Today, however, it stands as a shining tribute to renewal and renovation, as the formerly empty and decrepit old warehouses and brownfield sites have been converted into expensive loft flats, and along with those have come the Siamese triplets of such developments, expensive restaurants, open-air cafés and smart bars. A waterside footpath connects pricey apartment complexes with dozens of entertainment options, all close to the town centre. **Granary Wharf**, for instance, is just a few minutes from the train station, and is filled with bars and restaurants. It's worth visiting just for its Gothic-style architecture alone. Much further along the canals off Crown Point Road on Armouries Drive stands one of Leeds' best museums, the **Royal Armouries** ① *Clarence Dock, T0113-220 1999, www.royalarmouries.org.uk, daily 1000-1700, free.* Designed to hold the armour and weaponry from the Tower of London, it has been cleverly expanded into an interactive museum with a

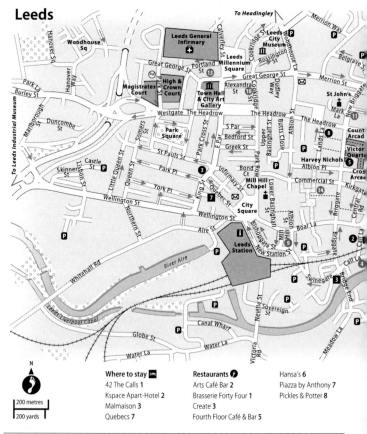

Leeds

Where to stay 🛏
42 The Calls **1**
Kspace Apart-Hotel **2**
Malmaison **3**
Quebecs **7**

Restaurants 🍴
Arts Café Bar **2**
Brasserie Forty Four **1**
Create **3**
Fourth Floor Café & Bar **5**

Hansa's **6**
Piazza by Anthony **7**
Pickles & Potter **8**

educational collection that spans 3000 years. There are excellent displays, costumed demonstrations, dramatic interpretations and live action events daily, along with well-made films and hands-on technology.

In the suburbs

Northeast of the centre is the Roundhay Park, one of biggest city parks in Europe covering nearly 300 ha, with gardens, woodland and a lake. In the park is **Tropical World** ① *T0113-395 7400, www.leeds.gov.uk, Apr-Oct 1000-1800, Nov-Mar 1000-1600, £3.30, under-16s £2.20*, with a large collection of tropical plants, the largest in the UK outside Kew Gardens. There aren't loads of animals to see here but there's a butterfly house, some lemurs and meerkats and by the time this guide is published there will also be a crocodile enclosure.

Three museums lie on the fringes of Leeds. The **Leeds Industrial Museum** ① *Armley Mills, Canal Rd, T0113-263 7861, www.leeds.gov.uk, Tue-Sat 1000-1700, Sun 1300-1700, bank holiday Mon 1000-1700, £3.30, concessions £1.70, under-16s £1.20, 2 miles west of Leeds City centre off the A65, from the centre take bus No 5, 733, 734, 735 or 736, or take a train to Burley Park, 1 mile from the museum*, has an unpromising name, but actually offers an interesting look at the city's past. The museum is located in a 17th-century mill, once the world's biggest woollen mill, and it tells the tale of the development of industry in Leeds, and in Britain as a whole. It delves into the development of the textile industry, and has hands-on exhibits, a 1920s working cinema and a century-old steam locomotive. The **Thackray Medical Museum** ① *Beckett St, T0113-244 4343, www.thackray museum.org, daily 1000-1700, £7, concessions £6, child £5, 2 miles northeast of the city centre, take bus 16, 42, 49, 50, 50A and 61*, is an enormously amusing place, with an entertaining display on the history of medical technology. Clearly designed to make medicine more interesting than frightening, it still has a serious bent and can get a bit grotesque at times. But it's all in the spirit of fun, and kids have a great time here. A few miles southeast of the centre is **Thwaite Mills** ① *Thwaite La, Stourton, T0113-276 2887, www.leeds.gov.uk, Sat-Sun 1300-1700, school holidays and bank holiday Mon Tue-Fri 1000-1700, £3.30, under-16s £1.20, bus No 110, 2½ miles from Leeds Station*, a working watermill on an island

Pubs & bars ①
Brewery Tap **9**
Nation of Shopkeepers **10**
North Bar **11**
Oporto **4**
Oracle **12**
Victoria **13**
Whitelocks **14**

near the Aire and Calder rivers. Also here is Thwaite House, showing how life was for the mill workers, and an engineer's workshop. There are some good riverside walks.

East of Leeds

Just 3½ miles outside the city centre off the A65, the walls of **Kirstall Abbey** ① *T0113-230 5492, www.leeds.gov.uk, Apr-Sep Tue-Sun 1000-1630 and Sat-Sun 1000-1700, Oct-Mar Tue-Sun 1000-1600, bank holiday Mon 1000-1600, free, from the city centre take bus Nos 22, 33A or 757, the nearest train station is Headingley, 1 mile away*, stand gloomily in a 24 ha green park on the River Aire. Considered the best preserved of all the Cistercian houses in the north of England, Kirkstall was founded in 1152 by monks from Fountains Abbey looking for a place of their own. It has stood empty for nearly 500 years since Henry VIII shut it down, and so it is astonishing how intact it remains. Its church is particularly interesting, even with its collapsed tower. The Norman chapter house is nearly perfect, in defiance of time, while the 13th-century abbot's lodging is simply beautiful. On the last Sunday of the month between March and November an outdoor artisan market is held at Kirkstall Abbey, and there's a deli market every last Saturday of the same months.

The 12th-century gatehouse has been restored and turned into the excellent **Abbey House Museum** ① *T0113-230 5492, www.leeds.gov.uk, Tue-Sun and bank holiday Mon 1000-1700, open at 1200 on Sat, free*. It is mostly devoted to Victoriana, with toys and games and reconstructed Victorian streets with an eye for detail in its shops, cottages and homes.

About 4 miles off the A63, **Temple Newsam** ① *T0113-336 7461, www.leeds.gov.uk, Apr-Oct Tue-Sun and Mon in the summer holidays 1030-1700, Nov-Mar Tue-Sun 1030-1600, house £3.70, farm £3.30, house and farm £6, under-16s £2.70/£2.05/£3.70, bus No 950 runs here in summer, call Metroline T0113-245 7676, the nearest train station is Cross Gates, 1½ miles away*, holds an impressive collection of decorative art. The Tudor-Jacobean house is a bit of an artwork itself, and inspired Templestowe in Scott's *Ivanhoe*. Inside, the impressive collection includes pottery, silver and furniture from the 16th and 18th centuries. The house sits on farmland, with a rare breed farm, numerous gardens and a park laid out by the ever-busy Capability Brown. It's a popular and picturesque place for a picnic on a sunny summer day.

A few miles further east from here is **Lotherton Hall** ① *off Collier La, Aberford, T0113-281 3259, www.leeds.gov.uk, daily Mar-Oct 1000-1700, Nov-Feb 1000-1600, £5, concessions £4, child 2.50, bus Nos 64 or 64A then a 20-min walk, in summer No 950 runs to the house, the nearest train station is Garforth, 4 miles away*, which holds silver, porcelain, jewellery, period furniture, costumes and mostly minor paintings. The entire contents were once the belongings of one wealthy family. Much like Temple Newsam, the house is surrounded by lovely grounds with some good walking trails, gardens – including a bird garden – and a deer park.

North of Leeds

About seven miles north of central Leeds is the model village of **Harewood** and the mansion known as **Harewood House** ① *T0113-2181010, www.harewood.org, daily mid-Feb to Mar gardens and grounds 1000-1600, house state rooms closed, house below stairs 1100-1600, bird garden 1000-1500, Apr-Oct 1000-1800, house state rooms 1000-1600, house below stairs 1100-1600, bird garden 1000-1700, £14, under-16s £7, grounds and below stairs only £10, under-16s £6*. The house was built from 1759-1772 by a superteam of designers, landscapers and architects assembled by the respected Yorkshire architect

John Carr. The building was designed by Carr and modified and finished by Robert Adam, the gardens were created by Capability Brown and the furniture by Thomas Chippendale (who was born not far from here in Otley). Even when the building was remodelled 100 years later, it was by the best of the best – Sir Charles Barry (who designed the Houses of Parliament) remodelled the façade and added the third storey. The art inside is an astonishing collection that includes works by Titian, Tintoretto, Bellini, El Greco and Turner. Outside is an extensive bird garden with acres devoted to hundreds of species of exotic birds, and an adventure playground. Also on the grounds are the ruins of Harewood Castle and Harewood Church. In a bit of literary trivia, the church contains the tomb of Chief Justice Gascoigne, who died in 1419. In *Henry IV, Part II*, Shakespeare describes Gascoigne committing the future King Henry V for contempt of court.

Bradford and around

Another northern industrial town, Bradford is not known for its beauty, but it has some attractive sections that are often overlooked by those outside of Yorkshire, most of whom would never think of coming here as a tourist. That's a pity, as the city has a lot to offer. Some of its early 20th-century architecture is unique in this region. But this is a very modern town. Including its suburbs, it's the fourth largest metropolitan area in England, and remains a very lived-in city. While it has interesting tourist sights, it is not a tourist city by any means. It's a workaday modernized industrial community, which has been a bit of a latecomer to tourism. But if you don't mind the town hurrying by you as it goes about its business, there's much to be seen here. Now named a UNESCO City of Film, Bradford has much to offer in the way of cultural attractions, including its National Media Museum.

Arriving in Bradford
Tourist information Bradford TIC ⓘ *Britannia House, Broadway, T01274-433678, www.visitbradford.com, Apr-Sep Mon-Sat 1000-1700, Oct-Mar closes at 1600.* Offers helpful advice, more maps than you need, and more brochures than you might think possible. You can also download maps and brochures from their website.

Places in Bradford
The City Hall precinct on the inner ring road is a good place to start, with the Gothic **City Hall** built in the late 19th century, and the neoclassical **St George's Hall**, dating from 1853 and dominating the corner of Bridge Street. Both buildings were designed by the same architecture firm, and yet each is very different from the other. Nearby the creamy columns of the **Alhambra Theatre** lure the eye with their pure linear structure, showing the transition of architectural mores from Victorian style to new modern lines at the time of its construction in 1914. Now beautifully restored, its interior is as gorgeous as its exterior. From the front of the theatre you can see the excellent **National Media Museum** ⓘ *T0844-856 3797, www.nationalmediamuseum.org.uk, daily 1000-1800, free,* the main reason why many visitors make their way to Bradford. Opened in 1983 and now with seven floors of exhibits, it holds the first IMAX cinema to open in Britain. Highlights include the National Photography Gallery, which traces the history of photography and displays equipment and numerous photos; the National Cinematography Collection, showing the history of cinema and amateur films; and collections on TV and digital media.

The Life Online Gallery is the latest addition and explores the history of the internet and its influence. You can spend hours here, so it's lucky there's a café and a bar for sustenance, and a shop filled with prints, movie posters and clever souvenirs.

Just north of the National Media Museum is **Bradford 1 Gallery** ① *T01274-437800, www.bradfordmuseums.org, Tue-Fri 1100-1800, Sat 1200-1700, free*, the city's modern art gallery hosting temporary exhibitions. Also here is **Impressions Gallery** ① *T01274-737843, www.impressions-gallery.com, same opening hours as Bradford 1 Gallery, free*, which showcases contemporary photography.

East of here, the Gothic **Wool Exchange** on Market Street – once again by Lockwood and Mawson, who designed the City Hall – is one of few indications you'll find around town that Bradford was once the world's largest producer of worsted cloth and woollen items. The old exchange has been beautifully renovated and converted into a small shopping and dining mall. Above the exchange, the tower of the beautiful **Bradford Cathedral** stands on nearby Stott Hill. The 14th-century building was much altered during the 20th century, but still contains a 15th-century font cover and 19th-century stained glass in the Lady Chapel. Opposite the Wool Exchange stands the **Peace Museum** ① *10 Piece Hall Yard, T01274-780241, www.peacemuseum.org.uk, Thu and Fri 1000-1600, free but donations welcome,* a one-of-a-kind facility with informative displays devoted to world leaders who espouse non-violence, tactics by which violence can be avoided, and conflict resolution.

In Lister Park, 1½ miles north of the centre is **Cartwright Hall** ① *T01274-431212, www.bradfordmuseums.org, Tue-Fri 1000-1600, Sat-Sun 1100-1600,* the city's civic art gallery which has mainly 19th- and 20th-century art from the UK, with some Southeast Asian contemporary art.

There are several museums at the edge of Bradford that can warrant a visit. The **Bradford Industrial Museum** ① *Moorside Rd, Eccleshill, T01274-435900, www.bradford museums.org, Tue-Fri 1000-1600, Sat-Sun 1100-1600, free,* for example, has an outstanding display on the city's industrial past. Built inside a converted 19th-century worsted spinning mill, the museum also features a recreated industrial neighbourhood with mill stables and shire horses, a mill owner's house and worker cottages. There are horse-pulled bus rides and daily demonstrations of spinning techniques, and on Wednesdays, steam looming machinery is fired up and operated. Four miles west of the town centre is the former parsonage where Charlotte, Branwell, Emily and Anne Brontë were born, at 72 Market St, Thornton, which is now a privately owned house.

Saltaire

Just at the edge of Bradford off the A650, Saltaire is a fascinating model village designed by a 19th-century mill tycoon (Sir Titus Salt) who sought to create the perfect industrial world. When Salt moved his mills from Bradford to the countryside, he decided that industrial didn't have to mean 'ugly', and so he created a village based on the architecture of Italy, which he loved. He built terraced housing with an Italian Renaissance look. He chose the countryside so that workers would breathe fresh air, rather than pollution. Today, sadly, Bradford's sprawl has wrapped around Saltaire, so the fresh country breezes are no more but still, it's an extraordinary place, as recognised by UNESCO who have designated the town a World Heritage Site. There is a **tourist information office** ① *2 Victoria Rd, T01274-437942, saltaire.vic@bradford.gov.uk, Mon-Sat Apr-Sep 1000-1700, Oct-Mar 1000-1600.*

The massive **Salts Mill** ① *T01274-531163, www.saltsmill.org.uk, Mon-Fri 1000-1730, Sat-Sun 1000-1800, free* is designed like an overgrown Italian *palazzo*, but don't be fooled by its beauty as this was a workhorse of a building. It once contained more than 1200 looms. Today, somewhat unsurprisingly, it's an upscale shopping centre filled mostly with art boutiques. Its largest tenant is the **1853 Gallery**, which is devoted to the works of David Hockney, the artist born in nearby Bradford, and it also has an interesting exhibition on the history of Saltaire. Around the mill, Salt built up the community for his workers in houses of different sizes based on the position of the worker who lived there, schools, hospitals and baths. Today it's a pretty and perfectly organized town – too perfectly organized, in fact. It's almost eerily unblemished. Appropriately enough, the man who's vision this all was, had himself buried at the centre of his town: Salt is in the mausoleum by the Italianate **United Reformed Church** ① *T01274-597894, www.saltaireurc.org.uk, Easter-Oct daily 1400-1600, Oct-Easter Sun 1400-1600, services at 1030 on Sun*, which was built in 1859 by Lockwood and Mason, who designed many of Bradford's most impressive buildings.

Just outside of the town centre, follow the signs across the Leeds–Liverpool Canal along Victoria Road to **Shipley Glen Tramway** ① *T01274-589010, www.shipleyglen tramway.co.uk, Sun 1200-1630, £1, concessions 50p*, where a Victorian cable tram travels up a steep wooded hill, where there is the Bracken Hall Countryside Centre, with displays on the geology and natural history of the area. At the base of the hill is a small museum about Shipley Glen and the tramway.

Haworth

Whatever Haworth once was, today it is Brontë country. The little village at the edge of the Pennines has long ago had its way of life subsumed by the world's seemingly limitless curiosity about these reclusive, rural sisters who wrote tales of repressed passions on heather-strewn moors. In 1820, when Anne, Emily and Charlotte were still small, their father moved them and their three other siblings from the edge of Bradford where they'd been born, to this stony village at the edge of miles of hills and sweeping vistas. Here they would grow up, and all of them would see their work affected by the stark, dramatic countryside around them. It seems that every street they once walked on and every building they ever entered, has been turned into some sort of Brontë memorial, but the biggest is the **Brontë Parsonage Museum** ① *T01255-642323, www.bronte.org.uk, daily Apr-Sep 1000-1730, Oct-Mar 1100-1700, £7, concessions £6, under-16s £3.60*, at the top of the main street. Located in the simple house in which they grew up, the displays inside tell the family's sad tale. The house is filled with pictures of the children, and the furniture remains the same as it did when they lived here. There are are extensive original documents written by the girls, starting when they were children and working up to their successful novels. This is a good museum, but crowded in the high season. The poet Ted Hughes grew up near Haworth and wrote about walking in the footsteps of the Brontës, as so many do here every year.

Also popular is the **parish church** adjacent, in which all of the family, except Anne (who is buried in Scarborough, see page 59) are entombed in the family vault. Nearby is the **Sunday school** where the sisters taught when they weren't writing and down the road is the former pharmacist where their brother Branwell bought the opium to which he was addicted. The **Black Bull Inn**, where he often drank himself into a stupor, is still open for business.

The countryside around Haworth is beautiful, and there are numerous **walks** along the paths that so inspired the Brontës. The **tourist office** ① *2-4 West La, at the top of Main St, T01535-642329, haworth.vic@bradford.gov.uk, daily 0930-1730*, will give you maps and directions. The most interesting of the walks is the one to **Top Withens**, a ruined, gloomy building out in the hills that many determinedly believe was the model for *Wuthering Heights*. Aside from the desolate nature of the countryside there, the windswept hills and the heather, there is no reason to think so, according to Brontë scholars, who say the buildings do not now and never did look the way Emily described them in her book. Further along, though, is **Ponden Hall**, which could well have been the building she called Thrushcross Grange in her novel.

Hebden Bridge and Heptonstall

A few miles south of Haworth, the A646 dips into the valley of the River Calder, and the Pennine Way walking path crosses the road by the stark **Stoodley Pike obelisk**, which makes for sweeping photographs. Nearby sit the twin tiny mill towns of **Hebden Bridge** and **Heptonstall**. In the 19th century, when these were bustling towns producing enormous amounts of textiles, the mills in Hebden Bridge ran constantly, while the workers lived up the hill in Heptonstall. The mills were long ago silenced, but the two towns are still connected by a path that once was used by packhorses moving fabric and wool.

Bohemian Hebden Bridge is well known for its larger-than-average alternative population; over the past 40 years the town has become a magnet for artists, writers and alternative therapists and it also has a substantial gay community. In 2013 it was voted the number one coolest place to live in Britain by *The Times*. The influx of creative, liberal-minded people explains why there are more independent, vegetarian and organic cafés and restaurants, and cultural venues, as well as a vibrant music and arts scene, than other market towns of this size. The town has a rare working **clog mill** ① *Walkley's, Midgley Rd, Mytholmroyd, T01422-885757, www.clogs.co.uk, Tue-Fri 1000-1700, Sat 1000-1600*, that is open to visitors. The sight of it groaning into life offers an interesting perspective on how life must have once been in this section of Yorkshire when hundreds of such mills ran nonstop. You can also buy clogs at their shop.

Heptonstall is a handsome village, much less crowded with tourists than Haworth (as the Brontës never came here). At its centre is an old ruined church, as well as a slightly newer (18th-century) Wesleyan chapel. But its main draw is the grave in the newer of its two churchyards in which the American poet Sylvia Plath lies buried. Her husband, Ted Hughes, was born in nearby Mytholmroyd and grew up in and around Heptonstall. He frequently wrote about the towns, not the least in the poem 'Heptonstall Churchyard'.

Halifax

One of the biggest towns that grew out of the worsted wool trade that dominated this section of Yorkshire for hundreds of years, Halifax clings for dear life to a hillside leading down into the Hebble valley. Over the years, its importance waned with the Yorkshire wool industry; but today its most interesting sites are virtually all tied to the textile industry in which it once had such success. The **tourist information office** ① *inside Piece Hall, T01422-368725, halifax@ytbtic.co.uk, daily 1000-1700*, can help you book a room or find good local walks.

Places in Halifax

The biggest memorial to the town's wool heritage is the central colonnaded **Piece Hall** ① *T01422-349422, www.thepiecehall.co.uk*, which was built in 1779 as a trading market for the wool industry. The only surviving cloth hall in Yorkshire (and it was very nearly torn down in the 1970s) its sheer size – covering over 8000 sq m – is a good indication of just how enormous that industry was at the time of its construction. These days it holds dozens of art shops and clothing boutiques, as well as the tourist information office (see above). There's also a colourful open-air market in the hall's vast courtyard on Fridays and Saturdays. At the time of writing it was about to undergo a massive multi-million pound transformation in late 2013, turning into a new tourist attraction with a heritage centre by 2015. This will replace the old Pre-industrial Museum and Calderdale Industrial Museum, which told the story of the rise and fall of the Yorkshire wool and cloth industry.

The town's own version of the guillotine was called a gibbet. So ferocious was the town's anti-crime bent and so enthusiastic its use of the gibbet that criminals used to joke darkly 'From Hull, hell and Halifax, good Lord deliver us'. A reconstructed gibbet stands in **Gibbet Street**, where the real device once did its bloody work. The jagged spire that juts up behind the Piece Hall is the only surviving part of the 19th-century Square Church, which long ago burned down. The nearby 17th-century **Square Chapel** ① *T01422-349422, www.squarechapel.co.uk*, has been converted into an arts centre and is the site of regular performances by touring international dance and theatre companies.

The town has a number of strikingly beautiful 15th- and 16th-century houses, which reflect the rise of the yeoman class of clothiers, who took in the wool from several workers, and thus grew in wealth. Among the most beautiful of these houses is the half-timber **Shibden Hall** ① *Lister's Rd, T01422-352246, www.calderdale.gov.uk, Mar-Nov Mon-Sat 1000-1700, Sun 1200-1700, Dec-Feb Mon-Sat 1000-1600, Sun 1200-1600, £3.50, under-16s £2.50, family £10*, off the A58 about a mile east of the town centre. The large 15th-century house stands in a gorgeous 37 ha park above a lake and has been converted into a museum filled with period furniture and late 16th-century paintings.

South and West Yorkshire listings

Sheffield p72, map p74

£££-££ Hilton, Victoria Quays, T0114-252 5500, www3.hilton.com. With a location on the canals and great views. There are usual luxuries, including a 20-m-long indoor pool, gym, sauna and therapy rooms.

££ Leopold Hotel, 2 Leopold St, T0114-252 4000, leopoldhotel.co.uk. Centrally located stylish hotel in a well-restored former grammar school dating from 1800. Smart rooms have flatscreen TVs, iPod docks and free Wi-Fi.

££ Number Fifteen B&B, T0114-327 6875, numberfifteensheffield.co.uk. This B&B in a Victorian house is in a good location in the attractive Westside district, near the Botanical Gardens.

££-£ Houseboat Hotels, Victoria Quays, T01909-569393, www.houseboathotels.com. Well located right on the canal, this is the city's most unusual place to stay, on one of 2 comfortable houseboats. Guests can use the pool and gym at the **Hilton** opposite.

Leeds p76, map p79

With its universities and busy business centre, Leeds has plenty of places to stay. Most expensive places are in the town centre, while most B&Bs are in the Headingley neighbourhood, easily accessible by bus.

£££ 42 The Calls, 42 The Calls, T0113-244 0099, www.42thecalls.co.uk. If the name is the same as the address, you can almost guarantee it's going to be stylish and expensive. This modern hotel in a converted corn mill overlooking the waterfront fits the bill on both counts and is the hottest hotel in town. Weekend packages can make it slightly more affordable. Free Wi-Fi.

£££ Malmaison, 1 Swinegate, T0844-693 0654, www.malmaison.com. Upmarket large hotel in the grand edifice of what used to be the city's transport company HQ. It's the perfect place to be pampered after a hard day's shop at Leeds' designer boutiques.

£££ Quebecs, 9 Quebec St, T0113-244 8989, www.quebecshotel.co.uk. Another of Leeds' posh boutique hotels in a fabulous Victorian Gothic building with luxurious rooms and suites. Wi-Fi, parking and entry to a nearby gym and spa are included.

££ Kspace Apart-Hotel, Waterloo Court, T870-199 8092, www.kspace-apartments.co.uk. Luxury studio, 1- and 2-bed self-catering apartments in Brewery Wharf. Minimum stay 2 nights. Parking and free Wi-Fi.

Bradford p81

Most accommodation is near the town centre, but there are many good B&Bs in the small towns nearby or in Haworth.

££ Great Victoria Hotel, Bridge St, T01274-728706, www.victoriabradford.co.uk. Lush and individually decorated rooms in this Victorian hotel by the station. Free Wi-Fi and parking.

££ Mercure Bankfield Hotel, Bradford Rd, Bingley, T0844-815 9004, www.mercure bradford.co.uk. Less central but equally deluxe it's located in a gorgeous manor house with 103 elegant rooms where you can rest in style.

££ Midland Hotel, Forster Sq, T01274-735735, www.peelhotels.co.uk. The height of Victorian luxury and conveniently located near the train station. Rates include Wi-Fi and use of a nearby gym.

£ New Beehive Inn, 169-171 Westgate, T01274-721784, www.newbeehiveinn.co.uk. A charming, gaslit inn with Edwardian character and good-value rooms, a 10-min walk from the centre. Also has a great bar; see page 90.

Haworth p83

There are plenty of B&Bs in town, but they book up quickly, even in the low season, so plan well in advance. You can get a full list from the tourist office.

£££ Old White Lion Hotel, Main St, T01535-642313, oldwhitelionhotel.com. A picturesque, rambling old inn right next to the parsonage. It has 2 lovely old bars and a handy restaurant. Free Wi-Fi.

£££-££ The Old Registry, Main St, T01535-646503, www.theoldregistry haworth.co.uk. On the cobbled main street is this pretty guesthouse with individually decorated rooms, some with 4-poster beds and whirlpool baths.

£££-££ Weavers, 15 West La, T01535-643822, www.weaversmall hotel.co.uk. A lane of old weavers' cottages that have been converted into guestrooms, filled with antiques. There's also an excellent restaurant and bar here; see page 88.

££-£ The Apothecary, 86 Main St, T01535-643642, www.theapothecary guesthouse.co.uk. There are excellent views from the windows of this charming guesthouse in the centre of the village. Free Wi-Fi, gym and sauna.

Halifax p85

£££ Shibden Mill Inn, Shibden Mill Fold, Shibden, T01422-365840, www.shibden millinn.com. Attractive and elegant inn set in a wooded valley. Excellent restaurant.

££ Field House, Staups La, Stump Cross, T01422-355457, www.fieldhouse-bb.co.uk. B&B on a working farm in Shibden valley with lots of great walks starting from the house. The hearty breakfast uses farm produce.

££ Ploughcroft Cottage, 53 Ploughcroft La, T01422-341205, www.ploughcroft cottage.com. Just a few miles out of Halifax are these 3 18th-century crofters' cottages at the top of the hill overlooking Halifax.

🍴 Restaurants

Sheffield p72, map p74

£££-££ Rafters, 220 Oakbrook Rd, T0114-230 4819, www.rafters restaurant.co.uk. More upmarket and formal, with a good-value set menu for £25 Mon-Thu.

££ Milestone, 84 Green La, T0114-272 8327, www.the-milestone.co.uk. Great bar and restaurant set in an industrial cityscape. Dishes use locally sourced, seasonal and organic ingredients and they pride themselves on everything being homemade. Also runs the popular bar and restaurant, the **Wig and Pen** (www.the-wigandpen.co.uk, **££-£**), in Campo La in the city centre.

££ Nonnas, 535-541 Eccleshall Rd, T0114-268 6166, www.nonnas.co.uk. Closed Sun. A Sheffield institution, dishing up good-quality Italian classics.

££-£ Silversmiths, 111 Arundel St, T0114-270 6160, www.silversmiths-restaurant.com. Tue-Thu from 1730, Fri-Sat from 16.45. City centre restaurant in a former cutlery works with a Yorkshire menu focusing on produce from the local area. Pie night on Tue.

£ Blue Moon Café, 2 St James St, T0114-276 3443, www.bluemooncafesheffield.co.uk. Long-established popular café in a high-ceilinged, bright room providing a good choice of vegetarian and vegan fare, and fabulous cakes.

£ Fusion Organic Café, Arundel St, T0114-252 5974, www.academyof makers.co.uk. Mon-Fri 1000-1500, Thu-Fri 1800-2200. Like **Silversmiths** on the same street, this place is in a renovated cutlery factory, Butchers Works, and is one of the best cafés in Sheffield. The wood-fired oven is used for baking organic bread and cakes. It turns into a bistro 2 nights a week. Also here are craft workshops and a gallery.

Leeds p76, map p79

££ Brasserie Forty Four, 44 The Calls Hotel, www.brasserie44.com. Contemporary surroundings at this smart bar and restaurant with superb French-style food and extensive wine list. Prices are correspondingly on the high side.

££ Fourth Floor Café & Bar, Harvey Nichols, Briggate, T0113-204 8000, www.harvey nichols.com. One of the hottest places in town, this newly refurbished diner is now even swankier. It packs in shoppers and non-shoppers alike for modern lunch and dinner menus. The **Espresso Bar** serves impressively expensive morning coffee, lunches, snacks and afternoon tea downstairs in the Victoria Quarter.

££ Piazza by Anthony, Corn Exchange, T0113-247 0995, www.anthonys restaurant.co.uk. Taking up the entire ground floor in the Corn Exchange, this place is a restaurant, café, bar, cheese shop and bakery, all of which serve the best quality food for which chef Anthony Flinn is famous for in Leeds. In the Victoria Quarter is an offshoot: **Anthony's Patisserie**, a good pitstop while shopping.

££-£ Art's Café Bar, 42 Call La, T0113-243 8243, www.artscafebar.co.uk. Delicious food in a laid-back atmosphere at this unpretentious café. Artwork by local artists brightens the walls.

££-£ Create, 31 King St, T0113-242 0628, www.foodbycreate.co.uk. Excellent value modern British dishes at this bright restaurant which provides work for long-term unemployed trainees. It's run by Richard Walton-Allen, former head chef at Harvey Nichols.

£ Hansa's, 72-74 North St, T0113-244 4408, www.hansasrestaurant.com. Mon-Sat 1700-2200, Fri-Sat until 2300, Sun 1200-1400. This long-established Guajarati vegetarian restaurant is deservedly popular, with its all-female staff. Hansa's also run a cookery school here and have published their own cookbook. Recommended.

£ Pickles & Potter, 18-20 Queens Arcade, T0113-242 7702, www.picklesand potter.co.uk. You can pick some seriously good sandwiches here, as well as some excellent cakes to follow, at this friendly café.

Bradford *p81*

Bradford's curry restaurants are legion and renowned. If you don't fancy curry, however, you might be in a bit of trouble, as there's not much to choose from.

£ Karachi, 15-17 Neal St, T0274-732015. Bradford's best-known curry restaurant opened in 1953 and is still going strong. Despite its somewhat down-at-heel appearance it still dishes up one of the best curries in town.

£ Kashmir, 27 Morley St, T01274-726513. Established basement curry café and upstairs restaurant renowned for its good food at extremely reasonable prices.

£ Prashad, 137 Whitehall Rd, Drighlington, T0113-285 2037, www.prashad.co.uk. Gujarati-influenced vegetarian dishes, including some great little roadside snacks and a special meal for kids with no chillies. It also featured on Ramsey's Best Restaurant 2010.

£ Treehouse Café, 2 Ashgrove, T01274-732354, www.thetreehousecafe.org. Mon-Fri 1130-1530. Opposite the university and part of Bradford Centre for Nonviolence, this café is staffed almost entirely by volunteers, who cook and serve well-priced Fairtrade and organic vegetarian and vegan dishes.

Haworth *p83*

This is a very small village, so your choice is going to be quite limited. Pubs are the best option for lunch, such as the **Black Bull** on Main St.

££ Old White Lion Hotel, see Where to stay. This restaurant features a good seasonal Yorkshire menu. It can get quite crowded at lunchtime.

££ Weavers, see page 87. For a slightly more sophisticated meal in an atmospheric restaurant. Book ahead.

Halifax *p85*

The most picturesque pubs and restaurants in Halifax tend to be in the Sowerby Bridge area, where many hotels are also located.

££ Design House, Dean Clough, T01422-383242, www.designhouse restaurant.co.uk. In a restored mill complex, this fine dining option offers contemporary dishes served by efficient staff.

🎧 Pubs, bars and clubs

Sheffield *p72, map p74*

The Bath Hotel, 66-68 Victoria St, off Glossop Rd, T0114-249 5151, www.beerinthe bath.co.uk. Head here for a good pint of real ale in a glorious Victorian setting.

Devonshire Cat, Wellington St, www.devonshirecat.co.uk. Popular local with a huge choice of real ales and Belgian beers.

The Fat Cat, 23 Alma St, T0114-249 4801, www.thefatcat.co.uk. A great but tiny pub and microbrewery, the **Kelham Island Brewery** (www.kelhambrewery.co.uk). It's a very local joint quite a way out from the centre on Kelham Island.

Sheffield Tap, train station, www.sheffieldtap.com. Freehouse bar with a great choice of cask ales, located in a restored Edwardian railway dining room.

Clubs

This is the city that created the Arctic Monkeys, Pulp and Human League, so it's understandable that Sheffield's music and nightclub scene is legendary.

Harley, 334 Glossop Rd, T0114-2752288, www.theharley.co.uk. Featuring a great line-up of regular live music and DJs.

Leadmill, 6 Leadmill Rd, T0114-221 2828, leadmill.co.uk. Sheffield's oldest music venue and club and one of the city's best places to see a band.

Plug, 14-16 Matilda St, T0114-241 3040, www.the-plug.com. Popular live music venue with some good club nights.

Leeds *p76, map p79*

One thing you're unlikely to hear somebody say in Leeds on a Fri night is, 'There's nothing to do here.' This town lounges all day and parties all night, in proper university town fashion.

Brewery Tap, 18 New Station St, www.brewerytapleeds.co.uk. Near the station, this place sells their very own Leodis lager, which is brewed on site.

Nation of Shopkeepers, 25-37 Cookridge St, T0113-203 1831, www.anationofshop keepers.com. Quirky bar with bunting, art on the walls, real ales, DJs and live music.

North Bar, 24 New Briggate, T0113-242 4540, northbar.com. Craft beer bar offering around 150 beers at a time, from around the globe, including the local Rooster from Knaresborough. Its sister pubs are in Northallerton (**Further North**) and in Water Lane (the **Cross Keys**).

Oporto, 33 Call La, T0113-245 4444, oportobar.co.uk. Lots of exposed brick, comfy sofas and relaxed vibes at this bar, which also has live bands and music nights.

Oracle, 3 Brewery Pl, Brewery Wharf, T0113-246 9912, www.oraclebar.com. If you fancy being a bit more sophisticated, sip a cocktail or glass of champagne at this slick bar with a terrace overlooking the waterfront.

Victoria, Great George St, T0113-245 1386, www.nicholsonspubs.co.uk. The only place for frilly Victorian pub life, near the Town Hall.

Whitelocks, Turk's Head Yard, T0113-245 3950, www.whitelocksleeds.com. One of Leeds' best-known pubs is worth a visit for its ornate historic pub decor, with lots of brass work and stained glass.

Clubs

Cockpit, Swinegate, T0113-244 1573, www.thecockpit.co.uk. Regular club nights and live music.

Hi-Fi Club, 2 Central Rd, T0113-242 7353, www.thehificlub.co.uk. Renowned Sat night comedy club, as well as club nights and live music.

The Wardrobe, Quarry Hill, T0113-383 8800, www.thewardrobe.co.uk. Live music venue which has hosted many big names since it opened in 1999 in its basement club. It's also a relaxed bar, with DJs and cocktails, and a restaurant. It was once used for storing theatre costumes, hence the name.

The Warehouse, 19-21 Somers St, T0113-234 3535, www.theleeds warehouse.com. A stalwart on the city's club scene, this place still plays the house tunes it's famous for, along with techno, dubstep and drum n bass.

Bradford *p81*

New Beehive Inn, see page 86. A friendly place for a drink with gas lamps, open fires and a good choice of real ales and imported beers.

Sparrow Bier Café, 32 North Parade, T01274-270772, thesparrowbradford.co.uk. Small bar offering beer on tap from local microbreweries in Ilkley and Kirkstall. Works by local artists adorn the walls and there are good food evenings, such as street food fridays, and occasional live music.

Halifax *p85*

The Navigation Inn, 47 Chapel La, Sowerby Bridge, T01422-316073, www.thenavigation pub.co.uk. A lovely pub for riverside drinking offering local real ales, in a plum location next to the Calder and Hebble.

Puzzle Hall Inn, Hollins Mill La, Sowerby Bridge, T01422-835547, www.puzzlehall.com. A friendly pub with a good selection of real ales and plenty of live music, including jazz, folk, acoustic and blues.

⚙ Entertainment

Sheffield *p72, map p74*

There are several theatres in Sheffield, all under the Sheffield Theatres Trust. The **Crucible**, **Crucible Studio** and **Lyceum** (T0114-249 6000, www.sheffieldtheatres. co.uk) theatres are all located around Tudor Square, and hold acclaimed performance by nationally known theatre groups and classical music on a regular basis.

Leeds *p76, map p79*
Cinema

Cottage Road Cinema, Headingley, T0113-275 1606, www.cottageroad.co.uk. The city's oldest cinema located north of the centre, still independetly run.

Everyman Cinema, Trinity Hall, T0871-906 9060, www.everymancinema.com. In the brand new shopping centre, the first Everyman venture outside of London.

Hyde Park Picture House, 73 Brudenell Rd, T0113-275 2045, www.hydeparkpicture house.co.uk. In the heart of studentland in Hyde Park is this beautiful Edwardian cinema showing arthouse films.

Music

Leeds Arena, Claypit La, T0844-248 1585, www.leeds-arena.com. Massive new music venue, due to open in Sep 2013. Elton John, JLS and Cirque Du Soleil are among those already booked in to perform.

Leeds Town Hall, The Headrow, T0113-224 3801, www.leedstownhall.co.uk. Classical music is performed frequently here in this glorious venue.

Theatre

City Varieties, T0113-243 0808, www.cityvarieties.co.uk. Historic Victorian music hall which now hosts comedy, music and panto performances.

Grand Theatre and Opera House, 46 New Briggate, T0844-848 2700, www.leedsgrandtheatre.com. This is where Opera North puts on a regular season of professional performances, alongside other touring productions.

West Yorkshire Playhouse, Quarry Hill, T0113-213 7700, www.wyp.org.uk. The best-known theatrical group in town, which puts on a range of highly rated performances, some of which go on to the West End.

Bradford *p81*
Cinema
IMAX, **Pictureville** and **Cubby Broccoli** cinemas, National Media Museum, see page 81. The UK's first ever IMAX screen, plus a 3D version. Pictureville and Cubby Broccoli screen arthouse classic and modern films.

Hebden Bridge *p84*
Cinema and theatre
Little Theatre, T01422-843907, hebden theatre.wix.com. Small but vibrant amateur theatre staging around 5 shows a year.
Picture House, New Rd, T01422-842807, www.hebdenbridgepicturehouse.co.uk. Historic 1920s cinema screening arthouse and latest release films. Also has live music and performances from stand-up comedians.

⊛ Festivals

Leeds *p76, map p79*
Aug Reading/Leeds Music Festival. Packs in hundreds of thousands of people in a field outside of town for a 3-day rock concert on Aug bank holiday weekend. See also www.leedsfestival.com.
Aug West Indian Carnival. A Notting Hill Carnival of the north.
Nov Leeds International Film Festival. This gets the local film buffs lining up for tickets on an annual basis. See leedsfilm.com.

Hebden Bridge *p84*
Hebden Bridge hosts an impressive range of festivals, including the **Handmade Parade** (22 Jun 2013), which features a procession with stilt walkers, a samba band and hand-made masks, costumes and giant puppets.

⊖ Transport

Also contact **Traveline**, T0871-200 2233, www.yorkshiretravel.net, for local public transport information.

Sheffield *p72, map p74*
Bus
National Express, T08717-818178, www.nationalexpress.com, services to **London** (4 hrs), **Leeds** (1 hr), **York** (2 hrs 30 mins), **Manchester** (3 hrs 15 mins), **Liverpool** (3 hrs) and many other cities.

Train
There is a regular service to **Leeds** (1 hr), **London** King's Cross (2 hrs 30 mins) and York (1 hr).

Leeds *p76, map p79*
Bus
The **Metro Travel Centre** at the bus station can get you going in the right direction (Mon-Fri 0830-1730, Sat 0900-1630) and advise you which travel card will work for you. **Metroline**, T0113-245 7676, has free bus travel advice for the confused and lost.

National Express, T08717-818178, www.nationalexpress.com, services to **London Victoria** (4 hrs 10 mins) every 30 mins, **Manchester** (1 hr to 1 hr 45 mins), **York** (45 mins), **Birmingham** (2 hrs 20 mins), **Sheffield** (1 hr) as well as many other destinations.

Train
Leeds is served by regular trains to **London King's Cross** (2 hrs 15 mins), **Birmingham** (2 hrs), **Liverpool** (2 hrs), **Manchester** (1 hr), **Sheffield** (1 hr) and **York** (25 mins).

Bradford *p81*
Trains run to **Saltaire** from Bradford's Forster Square, as does bus No 662. Trains also run direct to **Hebden Bridge** (30 mins).

Haworth *p83*
Train
The **Keighley and Worth Valley Railway**, T01535-645214, www.kwvr.co.uk, runs a steam train from Keighley to Oxenhope, stopping at Haworth. You can catch trains to Keighley from Leeds and Bradford and then switch to the steam train. It costs £14 for a day rover.

 Directory

Sheffield *p72, map p74*
Hospitals **The Royal Hallamshire Hospital**, Glossop Rd, T0114-271 1900.

Leeds *p76, map p79*
Hospitals **Leeds General Infirmary**, Great George St, T0113-2432799.

Contents

Yorkshire Dales

The western equivalent of the North York Moors, the Yorkshire Dales are just as beautiful and, if anything, even more dramatic. Seeing one without taking in the other is like hearing half the story. The word 'dale' comes from the Viking word for valley and while the moors are marked by gently rolling hills layered one upon another, the dales are more rugged, the hills steeper and more frequent, culminating in the three peaks of Pen-y-ghent, Ingleborough and Whernside. Amidst it all are the charming villages of Wensleydale, the arrogant beauty of Harrogate and historic Ripon and Richmond.

Visiting the Yorkshire Dales

Getting there and around The best **rail** access into the Dales is via the **Settle to Carlisle Railway** (www.settle-carlisle.co.uk), which offers glorious views into the bargain. There are connections to the line from Skipton and Leeds. By road from Leeds, the A65 provides easy entry to the Dales, heading through Ilkley or on to Skipton. From York, the A59 heads through Harrogate and on to Skipton. Once in the Dales, however, the most scenic route is on the small country **roads** that wind across the empty miles. The dales are well covered by **bus** services, especially in the summer, although service is patchy on Sunday and some holidays.

Tourist information See www.yorkshiredales.org.uk, for details of national park information centres. The main one is in Grassington; see page 96.

South Dales → *For listings, see pages 106-108.*

Ilkley

Heading into the dales from Leeds on the A65, the charming town of Ilkley is the first of any size that you come to. This allows the town to call itself 'the gateway to the dales'. One of several spa towns, the town's grand buildings owe their existence to Ilkley's 19th-century popularity among the upper classes (not much has changed) as a place to retreat for rest and 'healing' waters. Its best-known building is the dark grey **Manor House** ⓘ *T01943-600066, www.bradfordmuseums.org, Wed-Sat 1100-1700, Sun 1300-1600*. Built between the 15th and 17th centuries, it is reached through a stone archway from Church Street. It's been converted into a museum that traces the history of the village back to prehistoric times, and an art gallery. You can get walking maps from the **tourist information centre** ⓘ *opposite the train station on Station Rd, T01943-602319, Mon-Sat Apr-Sep 0930-1630, Oct-Mar 1000-1600*.

The countryside around Ilkley is fantastically dark and beautiful. The miles of heather on the **Ilkley Moor** are broken up by a number of ancient stone circles and hilltop crags. Unsurprisingly, there are many well-marked walks around the village, with two particular favourites: one to the **White Wells** – a whitewashed stone cottage built in 1756 around a moorland spring favoured by the infirm for its health-giving properties – and the other to the **Cow and Calf Rocks**, craggy hilltops that offer views that stretch for miles.

Skipton

Just a few miles from Ilkley, the bigger town of Skipton is a bustling place whose name, which means 'Sheeptown', gives away what the main business here once was. **Skipton TIC** ① *Town Hall, High St, T01756-792809, skipton@ytbtic.co.uk, Mon-Sat Apr-Oct 0930-1630, Nov-Mar 0930-1600, first Sun of the month 1000-1600,* has lots of information.

Today it could be called Castletown as the well-preserved **Skipton Castle** ① *T01756-792442, www.skiptoncastle.co.uk, Mon-Sat 1000-1800, Sun 1200-1800, Oct-Feb daily until 1600, £7, under-16s £4.40, family £22.50,* is one of the town's biggest tourist draws. A castle has stood on this site since 1090, although most of the current structure was built in medieval times. The thick 14th-century walls have endured more than time. They have survived a three-year siege by Parliamentarians during the Civil War. So sturdy was the squat little fortification with its rounded battlements (in places, its walls are over 3 m thick), that Cromwell ordered the roof to be removed, as it had survived one bombardment after another. When the castle's owner, Lady Anne Clifford, later asked to replace the roof, he allowed her to do so, as long as it was not strong enough to withstand cannon fire. Today the buildings are so complete that you cannot help but get the feel for what life was like for the villagers who worked and lived in its shadow, and under its protection.

In front of the castle, at the top of the high street stands the **Church of the Holy Trinity**, which also was restored by the resourceful Lady Anne, and contains the Clifford family tombs with heraldic decoration, a 15th-century roof and an elaborate 16th-century chancel screen.

From here, if you turn left, you'll come to the old town, where medieval Skipton had its centre. The canals and stone buildings here cry out for photos to be taken, in particular those around the **High Corn Mill**, the watermill that has been here so long it is mentioned in the *Domesday Book*. It still works, although it's now a shopping centre. Below the castle and the old town, Skipton is still a market town, as it has been for centuries. Its four weekly **market days** – Monday, Wednesday, Friday and Saturday – are events that bring in people from throughout the area. Its Christmas markets are particularly colourful and busy. Further down the High Street the old town hall has converted its first floor into the **Craven Museum & Gallery** ① *Town Hall, T01756-706407, www.cravenmuseum.org, Apr-Sep Mon, Wed-Thu, Fri-Sat and first Sun of the month 1000-1600, free,* which is packed with lots of interesting folk history, archaeological finds and geological displays from the area around Skipton, which is known as Craven. It also has art and costumes.

Bolton Abbey

① *T01756-718000, www.boltonabbey.com, Nov to mid-Mar 0900-1800, mid-Mar to May and Sep-Oct 0900-1900, Jun-Aug 0900-2100, £7 per vehicle.*

This is another one of those towns that has taken its name from an old monastery. In this case, unlike in some towns, at least the abbey ruins still exist. In fact, the scant remains of the **Bolton Priory** are the primary attraction here. The priory once formed part of a wide-ranging Augustinian network of churches and monasteries throughout the region. The building was started in 1150, and stood complete until the Dissolution when it was abandoned. The ruins were once much bigger – it was painted by Turner – but now all that remains is the nave, which has survived in good nick because it was used as the parish church for years. Aside from the priory, there's not much in Bolton, except the beginnings of a variety of **walks** through the lovely **Wharfedale** countryside and along the riverbanks. You can follow the path known as the **Strid** which wanders from the abbey for 4 miles alongside the river to the **Barden Bridge**, where **Barden Tower** stands as a further monument to the good works of Skipton's medieval conservationist, Lady Anne. It was used by Henry, Lord Clifford (known as the 'Shepherd Lord') for his alchemical studies during the reign of Henry VII. There's no gold here, but there is a tearoom where you can take sustenance before heading back, or you can continue on to the aptly named **Valley of Desolation**, with its gloomy beauty and waterfalls.

Grassington and around

Heading north from Bolton Abbey on the B6160 into an old lead-mining region, there's one tiny charming dales village after another. First is the adorably named village of

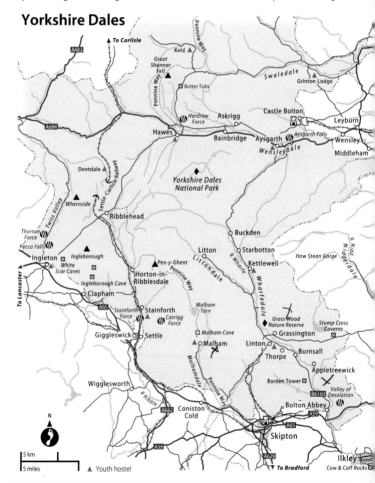

Yorkshire Dales

▲ Youth hostel

Appletreewick, which is nothing but cute, followed by the tiny village of **Burnsall**, which has an exquisite setting along a burbling stream. A few miles from there is **Grassington**, one of the bigger villages in the dales. Built by a picturesque river, Grassington is too big to be really pretty, but it has a mix of handsome touches overshadowed by a slight twee factor. The best part of the town is the setting, with the **Grass Wood Nature Reserve** providing a backdrop to the Georgian houses and the cobbled streets.

Grassington also has the main **National Park Information Centre** ⓘ *Hebden Rd, T01756-751690, grassington@yorkshiredales.org.uk*, where you can get help booking a room, find maps for walks in the area and explore the history of Wharfedale. You can drive the few miles from Grassington to the scenic village of **Linton**, with its lovely parks. This is a fantastic place for a picnic on a summer's day. Its small stream is crossed by both an ancient packhorse bridge and an old clapper bridge, and with its perfect 12th-century church, it is the picture of bucolic peace.

Around Malham Village

Due west of Linton you cross from Wharfedale into **Malhamdale** and enter one of the prettiest regions of the dales. The heather is permeated more frequently by limestone here, as this is a rocky region of striking high stone cliffs. It's a favourite with walkers, and the **Pennine Way** wanders through here, bringing a steady stream of ramblers. The biggest and busiest hub for these backpack toters is Malham Village. In the summertime, you simply cannot move for the walkers in this tiny village with its quaint stone cottages. In fact, by some estimates, half a million people a year make their way here. That means that, unless you are using this town as a setting off point yourself, there's too much of a crush here for it to actually be pleasant. If you're walking, there's a handy car park where you can leave your car and set off, and there's a **National Park Information Centre** ⓘ *T01729-833200, Easter-Oct daily 1000-1700, Nov-Easter Sat, Sun 1000-1600*, stocked with maps and advice on where to stop off on a multiple-day hike. The main attraction here, aside from the pub meals and comfy B&B rooms, is the proximity to nearby walking trails. Walking north on a well-marked path you can travel about a mile to the absolutely stunning **Malham Cove**, the misnamed geological formation along the Mid-Craven Faultline created by movement of the earth's plates, it is a massive limestone amphitheatre that towers hundreds of feet above the beautiful surrounding countryside. Another walk will take you to the glacial **Malham Tarn**, a lake protected as a nature reserve and inhabited by crowds of birds and animals.

Settle

Heading just a few miles west from Malhamdale to Settle, you cross over into the dark, dramatic moors of **Ribblesdale**. Settle is the biggest village in this area, and the terminus of the gorgeous Settle–Carlisle rail line, which passes through some of the most consistently beautiful countryside in Britain. As Malham does in Malhamdale, Settle makes a popular base for walkers in Ribblesdale. With the added attraction of the railway, this small town can get quite crowded as well in the summer. And, similarly, there's not much here except B&Bs and pubs. Walkers usually head directly to the **tourist information centre** ① *in the town hall on Cheapside off the market, T01729-825192, settle@ytbtic.co.uk, daily 1000-1700*, to pick up maps and to get guidance from staff on the best walks around the village. The well-signposted train station is a few minutes' walk from the tourist office and the town centre.

For walkers, there is plenty to see; Ribblesdale is dotted with charming villages. The village with the best name, **Giggleswick**, is less than a mile away on the opposite bank of the River Ribble. Happily, it is just as adorable as its name, with a babbling river, green moors, and old stone buildings on its tree-shaded streets. The old town school was built in 1512, while the small domed chapel is more beautiful inside than out. Just across the bridge from Giggleswick there's an easy footpath along the river to the tiny village of **Stainforth** with its charming pubs. The nearby **Stainforth Force** creates natural swimming holes, and there's an old packhorse bridge nearby which makes for an irresistible photo opportunity. Or hike to **Catrigg Force**, a small but beautiful waterfall east of Stainforth.

Horton-in-Ribblesdale

Along with Settle, the old quarry town of Horton-in-Ribblesdale is one of the most popular stops for walkers in the Dales. Many of the deep carvings around the village were scratched into the stone when the Settle–Carlisle Railway was being built in the late 1800s. The deep cuts and rocky hills make the area around here one of the most unusual you're likely to see in the north of England. The very industry that once made this town ugly and utilitarian has, over time, created extraordinary vistas. You can get lunch and tourist information at the **Peny-y-Ghent Café**, which is also a **National Park Information Centre** ① *T01729-860333. May-Sep Mon, Wed-Fri 0900-17300, Sat-Sun 0800-1730, Oct-Apr Sat-Sun 0900-1730*. This is where hikers planning to tackle the famed **Three Peaks Walk** often gather beforehand for information, advice and camaraderie. The three peaks in question are the mountains **Pen-y-Ghent** (693 m) to the east, **Ingleborough** (723 m) and the highest point in Yorkshire **Whernside** (737 m). The walk is a gruelling path around all three that takes 12 hours and covers more than 25 miles. It is only for fit and experienced hikers. Most hikers register at the Pen-y-Ghent Café when they head out for the path, and check in when they return, as a safety precaution. Getting lost or getting hurt are possibilities up there, and you want somebody to know that you're missing. Each April dozens of true fanatics race over all three of the hills in the mad dash known as the **Three Peaks Race**. The fastest runners complete the whole circuit in three hours.

Clapham

Famed for its caves, the attractive little village of Clapham is a few miles due west from Horton-in-Ribblesdale at the foot of the Ingleborough. There's a car park at one end of the little town, where you're well advised to leave your wheels and strike out on foot like everybody else. Aside from climbers headed up the peak, the main draw here is in the other direction, down into the **Ingleborough Cave** ① *T01524-251242, www.ingleborough cave.co.uk, entry by 50-min tours on the hour every hour (in peak season tours are every 30 mins) Feb-Oct half term daily 1000-1600, during the holidays, the last tour is at 1700, Nov-Feb 1000-1500, £7, under-16s £3.50, family £18*. There's an easy footpath that travels the mile from town to the cave entrance. The cave is extraordinary, filled with dark chambers and passages. The ceiling and floor are lined with dangerous looking stalactites and stalagmites that glitter like daggers.

Heading up another mile or so past the cave, you'll come to **Gaping Gill**, a cavern that plummets more than 90 m down, with a waterfall that rushes over the edge. Along with the spectacular view, there are also ruins on the summit of an Iron Age fort, with standing walls and foundations of circular huts that have been dated to the first century BC.

Ingleton

The furthest west point in the dales, the charming village of Ingleton straddles the junction of two picturesque streams in a ravine crossed by a 19th-century railway viaduct. Although the town is lovely, as with other dales villages, most people who come here aren't here to see the village. They're just fuelling up for one of the nearby hikes. Before setting out, get maps and information at the Ingleton **tourist information centre** ① *by the car park on Main St, T01524-241049*. You can also get help on accommodation here as well. The most popular hike is the 1½-mile walk to the **White Scar Caves** which are, if anything, more spectacular than the Ingleborough Cave. An internal waterfall provides a constant rumble that grows to a roar as you get closer to it. A series of walkways have been erected to make the tour through the depths safer, but it's still a cave, so there's a section where the walls are only about 1 m apart, and another where they're less than 1.5 m high. A tour here is not for the unfit. At the centre is the huge **Battlefield Cavern** ① *T01524-241244, www.whitescar cave.co.uk, Feb-Oct daily from1000, Nov-Jan Sat-Sun open from 1000, entry by 80-min tours, last tour at 1600, £9.50, under-16s £6, family £26*, 90 m long and 30 m high.

The other popular walk from Ingleton is the **Falls Walk** which climbs more than 2 miles up the gorgeous **Twiss Valley**, with viewing stations to take in the breathtaking scenery of the **Pecca Falls** and **Thornton Force**. There's a farm at the top of the walk where you can get something to eat, and then a different path takes you back for a fresh perspective on it all.

East Dales

Litton to Kettlewell

Heading east from the Three Peaks, you enter **Littondale**, where more small villages and good walks can be found. Litton makes a good base for climbing Pen-y-Ghent, but be aware that the villages here are so tiny that it gets harder to find accommodation or restaurants, so either bring your own tent and provisions, or drive back to one of the larger villages at the end of the day. Just beyond Litton the countryside is particularly beautiful, with rolling hills and deep valleys. The village of **Starbotton** is so tiny that if you blink you will indeed miss it, but that would be a shame as its **Fox and Hounds** pub is legendary, with its stone floors, large fireplace that all but heats the place itself, and good food.

A few miles away is another tiny village, **Buckden**, which is home to a handful of useful B&Bs. By the time you get to the village of **Kettlewell** you're back in Wharfedale. This makes a particularly good base for exploring the countryside, as the town is more beautiful and less busy than places like Grassington. There are a handful of B&Bs in town, a **campsite** north of town at Fold Farm, (T01756-760886) as well as a couple of good pubs in the town centre.

Pateley Bridge

Heading into the eastern Dales, the focus remains on rural walks, gorgeous countryside and charming villages like little Pateley Bridge. Small this village may be, but it's extremely important for walkers interested in taking in the scenery. You don't have to go far, a short stroll takes you up to the ruins of the church of **St Cuthbert** perched overlooking it all from a nearby hilltop. The ruins are striking – a compelling combination of dark and beautiful – and the view of the surrounding moors is simply spectacular. But that's not enough for most visitors, so it's handy that the **tourist information centre** ① *18 High St, T0845-389 0179, pttic@harrogate.gov.uk, Easter-Oct only*, has maps, information, advice and guidance for those interested in striking out. Before you head off, staff in hand, stop in at the **Nidderdale Museum** ① *T01423-711225, www, nidderdalemuseum.com, Apr-Oct daily 1330-1630, school summer holidays and bank holidays daily 1030-1630, Nov-Mar Sat-Sun 1330-1630, £2, under-16s free*, which can help you brush up on local history, complete with a recreated Victorian schoolroom, shop and parlour.

The best walks start a short drive from the town centre. For instance, the **Stump Cross Caverns** ① *T01756-752780, www.stumpcrosscaverns.co.uk, Feb half term to Nov daily 1000-1730, Dec to Feb half term Sat-Sun and Christmas school holidays 1000-1600, £7, under-16s £4.50*, with spectacular caverns and stalactites, are about five miles west of Pateley Bridge. Or you could drive 5 miles east of town to the legendary **Brimham Rocks** ① *T01423-780688, www.nationaltrust.org.uk, daily 0800-dusk, parking £4 for up to 3 hrs*, a walk that takes you over hundreds of acres upon which thousands of these mysterious boulders sprout like weeds. The overall landscape is strange and beautiful, with stones incongruously towering over green moors. If you head 7 miles north from Patelely Bridge you'll reach **How Stean Gorge** ① *Tue-Sun 1100-dusk, £5.75, under-16s £3.50*, with its 1-km-long ravine, which is up to 20 m deep in places, and spooky caves. There is also a Via Ferrata here, along with other activities such as rock climbing, caving and kayaking, and a campsite.

Harrogate and around

Most people reach Harrogate from the west, which is unfortunate, as coming at it from the northwest is particularly beautiful (with the added attraction of stopping to take a photo of the sign for the wonderfully named nearby village of **Glasshouses**). The best known town in the Dales, everything Harrogate has it owes to water; a specific kind of water that rises from Tewit Well, to be precise. The sulphur springs were discovered in 1571 and the rest is history. In the spa boom of the 18th and 19th centuries, Harrogate soon rose to the top, and the town bloomed around the springs in an explosion of austere and grand architecture, befitting the class of those who flocked to the town to drink the water, soak in the water, be electrified in the water, and all the other strange things they did back then in the name of 'health'. Agatha Christie took the waters here while considering divorcing her husband during her disappearance in 1926.

Arriving in Harrogate

Getting there The train station is on Station Parade near the town centre. Harrogate is well located for access to the Dales. The bus station is just down the street from the train station, with local and regional services. ➤➤ *See Transport, page 108.*

Tourist information Harrogate TIC ① *inside the Royal Baths, Crescent Rd, T01423-537300, Apr-Oct Mon-Sat 0900-1800, Sun 1200-1500, Nov-Mar Mon-Fri 0900-1700, Sat 0900-1600.*

Places in Harrogate

So well preserved is the town that you can walk in the footsteps of 19th-century society starting at the **Royal Baths Assembly Rooms** on Crescent Road. Plunge right in by taking a bath yourself at the **Turkish Baths** ① *Parliament St, T01423-556746, www.turkishbaths harrogate.co.uk, sessions start at £14.50, or visit on a 1-hr guided tour on Wed at 0900, £3.50.* Just around the corner from the Turkish Baths is the **Royal Pump Room Museum** ① *Crown Pl, T01423-556188, www.harrogate.gov.uk, Mon-Sat and bank holidays 0930-1600, Sun 1300-1600, £3.75, under-16s £2.20.* It stands over the well that provides sulphurous water for the baths, and has been converted to include an interesting museum. The big building that stands across from the baths is the 19th-century **Royal Hall**, where those in town for the waters would catch ballets and symphonies in the evening. Down the road from the Pump Room, the **Mercer Art Gallery** ① *T01423-556188, www.harrogate.gov.uk, Tue-Sat 1000-1700, Sun 1400-1700, free,* just a short distance away on Swan Road, is in the oldest pump building in town and exhibits mainly 19th- and 20th-century art.

The beautiful parkland that stretches across town is called (wonderfully) **The Stray**, and has decorated Harrogate for hundreds of years, exactly as it does today. Other historic gardens are nearby at the gorgeous **Valley Gardens** and the showy **RHS Garden Harlow Carr** ① *T01423-565418, www.rhs.org.uk, daily Mar-Oct 0930-1800, Nov-Feb 0930-1600, £7.70, under-16s £3.85,* which combine to give the town its deserved reputation as the horticultural centre of the north.

Knaresborough

A worthwhile day trip from Harrogate, Knaresborough – just four miles away – may well be one of the most underrated cities in England. Sitting as it does in the shadow of its famous neighbour, it's not well known despite its dramatic location above the River Nidd, its well-preserved townhouses, traditional pubs and colourful gardens. Even the railroad viaduct that crosses the ravine makes for an extraordinary view. Along with the lovely setting, Knaresborough has a modest **castle** ① *T01423-556188, www.harrogate.gov.uk, Easter-Sep 1100-1600, £3.20, under-16s £1.75, includes the Courthouse Museum, 30-min tours are also available,* ruin in a most picturesque location, towering above it all on a desolate hilltop. The remains of the Norman castle are mostly limited to its keep, but it's worth a visit if only because of its historic importance, which is well documented in the **Courthouse Museum** in the Castle Yard, which has a recreation of a Tudor court room. Best of all, you can see the dark old tunnels that run under the castle. On the river bank is the strange **Chapel of**

Our Lady of the Crag, a mysterious shrine carved into the rocks – apparently around 1400 – that contains the figure of a knight. Across the river from the castle in the **Dropping Well Estate** is a mysterious cave that was once home to the famed 15th-century prophet known as Mother Shipton. She was said to have predicted many of the events of the subsequent 500 years, from the Great Fire of London to the phenomenon of world wars. **Mother Shipton's Cave** ① *Harrogate Rd, T01423-864600, www.mothershipton.co.uk, Feb-Mar Sat-Sun 1000-1630 (until 1700 in Mar), Apr-Oct daily 1000-1730, £6, under-16s £4,* is filled with strange memorabilia and spooks the punters. Also here is the quite cool **Petrifying Well**, where the natural lime-rich waters turn everything they touch to stone. People have been putting objects here for years – from clothing to toys – and they are petrified in just a few months.

Ripley

Just a few miles north from Knaresborough the little town of Ripley is another of those strangely compelling 'model villages' on the lines of Saltaire (see page 82). This one was designed by Sir William Amcotts Ingilby in the 1820s, based on the traditional designs of Alsace-Lorraine villages, apparently on a whim. It's just the look of the place, with its vivid flower gardens, European square and shops selling your basic Yorkshire woollens and lavender soaps, which are its main attractions. But the best part is **Ripley Castle** ① *T01423-770152, www.ripleycastle.co.uk, entry by guided tour only, Dec-Feb Sat-Sun 1100, 12.30, 1400; Apr-Oct Mon-Sat 11, 1230, 1400, Sat-Sun and school holidays tours hourly 1100-1500; Mar and Nov Tue, Thu, Sat-Sun 1100, 1230, 1400, also tailor-made children's tours Easter to early Nov Sat-Sun 1145 and 1345, garden daily 0900-1700, £9, gardens only £6, under-16s £5.50, £4,* which stands above it all, as if in disbelief. The fairly well-preserved castle has a 15th-century gatehouse, a 16th-century tower and a nifty man-made lake. Parts of the castle are stocked with armour, memorabilia and period furnishings. Like most of the castles in these parts, it has a Cromwell connection, as he spent his first night here after the battle of Marston Moor. From the castle, near the bridge, you'll come across the old **All Saints' church**, where the walls are still nicked and dented from musket balls. According to local lore, the damage happened when Royalist soldiers were executed against the wall after Marston Moor. The grounds include a walled garden and a deer park.

Fountains Abbey

① *T01765-608888, www.nationaltrust.org.uk, abbey and gardens, Mar daily 1000-1700, Apr-Oct daily 1000-1800, Nov-Feb Sat-Thu 1000-1700, £8.60, under-16s £4.50.*

It's difficult to decide what's more beautiful, the remains of the Cistercian abbey or the wooded setting in the valley of the River Skell. Surrounded by the water gardens known as **Studley Royal**, which were designed in the 19th century to complement the rambling, jagged ruins of the abbey, the whole scene is simply extraordinary, equalled only by the hillside ruins at Rievaulx (see page 41). Fountains Abbey was founded by a rebellious group of Benedictines from York in 1132, but was taken over by the Cistercians within three years. Over the next century it grew into the most successful of the Cistercian monasteries in England, and that is reflected in the size of the ruins that remain today, growing out of the hillside in castle-like proportions of stone turrets and archways. Unlike many other Yorkshire abbeys, the ruins here are very substantial, including much of the **nave**, and the pointed **arcade** towering above Norman piers. The filigree remains of the **Chapel of the Nine Altars** gives some idea of how extraordinary this building must have been when complete. The **dormitory** where the lay workers slept is still largely intact, and it's clear that it was once massive, as it would have needed to be in order to house the hundreds of workers who lived and worked here, alongside the monks. On the south side of the ruins, the old **warming rooms** can be seen, along with the massive fireplaces which gave the rooms their names. The enormous tower that hovers over all the ruins was added in the 16th century, but remains the only later addition of any substance amidst the 12th-century ruins. The building by the entrance is **Fountains Hall**, built in the 17th century by Sir Richard Gresham, who bought the property on which the abbey stood after the Dissolution, and cannibalized much of the stone for his home from the old abbey. Luckily, the next owner of the property, John Aislabie, was more sympathetic to the old building. He stopped the destruction of the abbey, and designed the stunning gardens that now surround it, with a mixture of flowers, woods, deer parks and lakes. The most unusual of the features designed by Aislabie is the water gardens that include ponds, cascades and lakes, all integrated perfectly into the wild, wooded landscape. Scattered around the grounds are the more affected addition of garden buildings (so popular in the 17th century) including the 'Temple of Piety' and a banquet house. There is also a restored corn mill with a good interactive exhibition. One building that does work is the 19th-century **St Mary's Church** which includes an approach through an avenue of limes that frame the view of the abbey from the church. Despite the occasional wrong note hit by enthusiastic owners over the years, the combined effect of ruins and gardens is breathtaking.

Ripon

The pretty town of Ripon sit a few miles from Fountains Abbey and about 11 miles north of Harrogate. For more than 1300 years, its main draw has been its small but exquisite **cathedral** ① *T01765-603462, www.riponcathedral.org.uk, daily 0830-1800, free*. From the outside, it looks much like any other parish church, but inside the architecture dates back to its foundation by St Wilfrid in 672. Even a decade before then, though, there was a monastery on this site, mentioned by the ancient historian Bede in his writings of that time. The labyrinthine crypt, with its arched passageways and mysterious shadows has been dated to that period, and is, without question, the most extraordinary part of the building. A number of relics, including the Ripon jewel (discovered in 1976 and dated back to the building's earliest years) are on display down here. The Danes destroyed the rest of that first building in the ninth century. The chapel was built in the 11th century, and much of the rest of the building dates from the 12th century, although the twin towers at either side are 13th-century structures. There are regular chamber music concerts, and the Ripon Cathedral Choir is justifiably famous, and any chance to catch one of their performances should be grabbed; see the website for details of what's on. There's also an annual celebration in honour of St Wilfrid, as a procession moves regally down the streets in his name on St Wilfred's Feast the Sunday before the first Monday in August.

If you happen to be in town at around 2100 you'll catch the charming and historic **Wakeman ceremony**, in which a horn is blown from each of the central market square's four corners, and in front of the **Wakeman's House** on one side of the market. This dates back to 886, when Alfred the Great first granted the town a charter, and presented Ripon with an ox's horn for the setting of its nightly watch. The person who blew the horn nightly was the wakeman, and, until 1637, a wakeman always lived in a house on the square.

Masham

After the cathedrals, abbeys and castles of the rest of Yorkshire, Masham, about eight miles north of Ripon, has a bit of an air of 'and now for something completely different'. For this is beertown, pure and simple. In fact, beer lovers make pilgrimages here to see for themselves the mecca of **Theakston's** ① *T01765-680000, www.theakstons.co.uk, Jan-Jun and Sep-Dec 1030-1630, Jul-Aug 1030-1730, £6.50, children 10 and over only £4, prices include a pint of beer or a soft drink,* breweries. Tours of the large breweries tell you the current ways and means of beer brewing, along with the history of brewers' mysterious recipes and rules. There's also an independent micro-brewer in town, the **Black Sheep Brewery** ① *T01765-680100, www.blacksheep brewery.com, visitor centre Mon-Thu 1030-1630, Fri-Sat 1000-2300, Sun 1000-1630, 1-hr tours £5.95, under-18s £3.95,* which offers tours of the microbrewery process. Both breweries have their own pubs if you fancy sampling their beer after a tour.

Jerveaulx Abbey and Middleham Castle

Just north of Masham, at the beginning of Wensleydale, the barely-there ruins of the Cistercian **Jerveaulx Abbey** ① *www.jerveaulxabbey.com, dawn-dusk daily, small donation requested,* are located more or less in the middle of nowhere. There's not much left of this monastery, which is now privately owned, but the setting is lovely, and the fact that it all feels so abandoned and forgotten is part of the attraction.

Northeast Dales

Wensleydale and around

Just north of Middleham, the old farming community of **Leyburn** is another charming village with busy markets, cobbled streets, and lots of 18th-century buildings. Many people come here just to stop for lunch at the cosy **Golden Lion inn** on the marketplace, and to watch the rural world go by. Similarly adorable is the little village of **Wensley**, just a mile or so away. The town after which the dale is named, Wensley has a lovely 15th-century bridge and a parish church that dates from the 13th century. Inside the church of the **Holy Trinity** the 16th-century choir stalls are elaborately carved with poppies, and it has a 14th-century brass relief of a priest.

A mile west of Wensley are the 14th-century ruins of **Castle Bolton** ① *T01969-623981, www.boltoncastle.co.uk, mid-Feb to Oct daily 1000-1700 (until 1800 during school holidays), £7.50, under-16s £6, gardens only £3, £2.* The starkly beautiful surroundings and the cold thick walls of the castle were once the only view that Mary Queen of Scots had, as she was held prisoner here for months in 1658. Most of the castle has been well restored – in particular, the great hall, Mary's bedroom and the dungeons, as well as the castle gardens outside – but the best part of it all are the sweeping views of the rolling Wensleydale hills from the top of the battlements. Daily activities include archery, falconry and hawk and owl displays.

Aysgarth and Askrigg

The hilltop village of **Aysgarth** is blessed with a gorgeous setting at the edge of the River Ure, which streams by on its limestone bed and then tumbles over impossibly picturesque **waterfalls**. In the summer, the little village fills with walkers, parking their cars, picking up maps at the **National Park information centre** ① *T01969-662910,* and striking up the surrounding hills. The paths are well marked, both the **Upper Falls** and the **Lower Falls** are a short walk from the town centre through thick woods. And the views are extraordinary. A few miles west is the village of Askrigg, which may look familiar if you watched the TV series of the James Herriott book *All Creatures Great and Small*, which was filmed here and around. Aside from looking for buildings you recognize, there are walks from here to the ruggedly beautiful **Whitfield Force** and **Mill Gill Force**, each well marked and fairly short – neither is more than a mile from the town centre.

The jewel-like town of **Bainbridge** is just a couple of miles southwest of Askrigg, and has a historic nightly ceremony in which a horn is sounded on the village green at 2200, to call travellers in from the surrounding moors. The haunting horn sound is extremely evocative, and if you hear it without getting goosepimples, you're harder than most. The best place to be when the horn sounds is the 15th-century coaching inn, the **Rose & Crown Hotel** (T01969-650225, www.theprideofwensleydale.co.uk), which has a magnificent pub and pleasant rooms (**££**).

Hawes

The little mountain town of Hawes is an unlikely tourist hub. It is home to just 1200 souls, isn't particularly pretty and is primarily a centre of business and shopping for nearby farmers. But it is also surrounded by hills and waterfalls that act like flame to a moth for hikers. At 244 m, Hawes claims to be the highest market town in Yorkshire, and its weekly market on Tuesday is crammed with cheeses and locally made jams and fresh butter. The **Wensleydale Creamery** ⓘ *Gayle La, T01969-667664, www.wensleydale.co.uk, Mon-Fri 0900-1600, Sat-Sun 0900-1630, the best time to see cheese making is 1000-1400, but check in advance, £2.50, under-16s £1.50*, is a regular stop for visitors to find out more about cheese making in the museum and to see it being done, before tasting and stocking up on cheese in the shop. Cheese has been made in Hawes since the Cistercians started making it here in the 12th century, and it is sold everywhere in town. Most people are here to walk, however, and the closest, and easiest walk, takes you from the **Green Dragon** pub, where you can take enter the path up to the somewhat disappointing and small **Hadraw Force** ⓘ *April to mid-Sep daily and last 2 weekends in Sep Sat-Sun 1100-1600, £3.20, under-16s £1.75*, which Turner visited and sketched in 1816. More difficult walks head up to the **Great Shunner Fell**, or to the natural wells known as the **Butter Tubs**. Before you head out, stop by the **National Park Information Centre** for maps and advice. It is located inside the town's converted railway station, along with the surprisingly good **Dales Countryside Museum** ⓘ *T01969-666210, daily 0900-1730, closed Jan, £4, under-16s free*, which has interesting displays on rural life in the Dales.

Richmond

Just at the edge of the furthest eastern border of the dales, and about eight miles from Castle Bolton, the splendid castle town of Richmond provides a fitting ending to the dales, with its market square, Georgian architecture and bright gardens. There is a **tourist information office** ⓘ *Friary Gardens, Victoria Rd, T01748-828742, daily 0930-1730*.

At the centre is an 11th-century **castle** ⓘ *T01748-822493, www.english-heritage.org.uk, Apr-Oct daily 1000-1800, Nov-Mar Sat-Sun 1000-1600, £4.70, under-16s £2.80*, which stands guard from a steep precipice above the river. Lore connects this castle to England's most famous mythical king, as King Arthur is said to lie in a nearby cave, waiting for the time when England needs him again. Unlike many Yorkshire castles, the gloomy walls of Richmond

Castle still hold many of its original Norman buildings including its gatehouse, keep (one of very few surviving Norman keeps in the country, and perhaps the eldest) and curtain wall. There are also dramatic views from the sheer cliffs atop which it stands.

Like the castle, Richmond retains many of its original features as well. The town's streets are still cobbled and its narrow medieval alleyways still wander confusingly in a spiderweb of walkways and streets. The desanctified 12th-century **Holy Trinity Church** now holds the **Green Howards Museum** ⓘ *T01748-826561, www.greenhowards.org.uk, Mon-Sat 1000-1630, Apr-Oct Sun 1230-1630, closed Jan, £3.75, children aged 13-18 years £1.50, under-13s £1,* which tells the story of North Yorkshire's Green Howards regiment. Also of interest is the small but perfectly formed **Georgian Theatre Royal** ⓘ *T01748-825252, www.georgiantheatreroyal.co.uk, 40-min guided tours run hourly mid-Feb to mid-Nov Mon-Sat 1000-1600, suggested donation £3.50.* Built in 1788, it is England's oldest theatre, only reopened to the public in 1963 after sitting derelict for a century, which is difficult to believe when you see its exquisite Georgian interior. The little **museum** at the back of the theatre is all good fun, with hands-on access to stage sets and costumes.

Right at the edge of Richmond stand the ruins of **Easby Abbey** ⓘ *www.english-heritage.org.uk, daily Apr-Sep 1000-1800, Oct-Mar 1000-1600, free.* There is an easy, well-marked path here from the town centre. The abbey was founded in 1152 and once was home to hundreds of Premonstratensian canons. There are few sights more beautiful than the jagged ruins of this abbey at sunset.

Yorkshire Dales listings

⊖ Where to stay

Skipton *p95*
£££ Coniston Hotel, Coniston Cold, T01756-748080, www.theconistonhotel.com. Set in acres of private parkland is this sprawling, beautiful hotel with its own lake.
££ Highfield Hotel, 58 Keighley Rd, T01756-793182, www.highfield guesthouse.co.uk. This small and centrally located hotel is very handy and affordable.
££ Skipton Park Guest 'Otel, 2 Salisbury St, T01756-700640, skiptonpark.co.uk. Friendly and good-value B&B.

Bolton Abbey *p95*
££££ The Devonshire Arms, T01756-710441, www.thedevonshirearms.co.uk. A gorgeous luxury manor house offering a Michelin-starred restaurant and individually decorated rooms with antiques. Rates include use of the spa – with pool, sauna and gym – and entry to Bolton Abbey nearby.

Around Malham Village *p97*
Because Malham is very popular, you will need to book ahead.
££ Lister Arms, T01729-830330, www.lister arms.co.uk. Historic pub overlooking the village green with a relaxing atmosphere and great food.
££ Tudor House, T01729-830301, www.malhamdalehotels.co.uk. Lovely B&B in a former railway station on the Settle to Carlisle line, 4 miles from Malham.
£ YHA Malham, T0845-371 9529, www.yha.org.uk. Very popular hostel.

Settle *p98*
There are plenty of B&Bs and inns here.
££ Golden Lion, Duke St, T01729-822203, www.thelionsettle.co.uk. Handsome coaching inn with lots of original features.
££ Plough Inn, in nearby Wigglesworth, T01729-840243, www.theploughat wigglesworth.co.uk. Village inn with great views and a fine restaurant.

Ingleton *p99*

There's quite a bit of accommodation to choose from, although booking ahead in the summer is essential.

££ Bridge End Guest House, Mill La, T01424-241413, www.bridge-end-ingleton.co.uk. Attractive spot next to the river in the middle of the village, with good-value rooms.

££-£ YHA Ingleton, T0845-371 9124, www.yha.org. Well-placed hostel for walkers in a Victorian building, with an outdoor pool.

Harrogate *p100*

Harrogate is filled with hotels and B&Bs for every budget. The best areas to trawl for a room are on King's Rd and Franklin Rd.

££££-£££ Rudding Park Hotel, Rudding Park, Follifoot, T01423-871350, www.rudding park.co.uk. A converted manor house just outside of town, one of the most elegant hotels in the area. It also has an excellent restaurant and gorgeous bar, as well as a spa, gym, cinema nd 18-hole golf course.

£££ Hotel Du Vin, Prospect Pl, T0844 736 4257, www.hotelduvin.com. Overlooking the Stray, this lovely hotel has all the usual Du Vin appeal and facilities such as a stylish cellar bar, billiards room and aptly enough for this town, a spa. Some rooms have monsoon showers and rolltop baths. Recommended.

££ Ascot House Hotel, 53 King's Rd, T01423-531005, www.ascothouse.com. For much of the glamour at less of the price, try this rambling, turreted house in lovely grounds and has a fabulous bar. Free Wi-Fi.

££ Fountains Guesthouse, 27 King's Rd, T01423-430483, www.fountains harrogate.co.uk. Friendly and family-run place 5 mins' walk from the centre offering rooms at a reasonable price. Free Wi-Fi and parking.

££ White Hart Hotel, Cold Bath Rd, T01423-505681, www.whitehart.net. In a Georgian mansion in the town centre, this slick hotel offers comfortable rooms, an excellent restaurant and the **Fat Badger** pub

serving good-value food (**££**). Parking (£5 per night) and free Wi-Fi.

Masham *p104*

££-£ Bivouac Bunk Barn, High Knowle Farm, Knowle La, T01765-535020, www.thebivouac.co.uk. Take your pick from a yurt, a timber frame 'shack' or dorm bed in a rustic chic bunk barn at this beautiful site next to woodland complete with a folly called Druid's Temple. Also on site is a great little café.

Bainbridge *p105*

££££ Yorebridge House, T01969-652060, www.yorebridgehouse.co.uk. If you fancy a splurge, this is the place to head for. The decadent rooms are all sumptuously decorated in different styles and some come with a hot tub. There's an elegant restaurant and a bar, too.

Hawes *p105*

££-£ YHA Hawes, T0845-371 9120, www.yha.org. Good modern hostel for walkers and families with great views over Wensleydale.

Richmond *p105*

£££ Millgate House B&B, T01748-823571, www.millgatehouse.com. Charming upscale B&B located in the centre and crammed with antiques. Also has a grand dining room and a gorgeous walled garden.

££ Tan Hill Inn, Reeth, 11 miles from Richmond, T01833-628246, www.tanhil linn.co.uk. Wonderfully atmospheric inn, famous for being the highest in England at over 500 m, so be prepared to be snowed in if the weather's bad. The sweeping views are stunning and it's a handy base for walking too, as it's on both the Pennine Way and the Coast to Coast walk. Also has dorms (**£**).

££ Whashton Springs B&B, Low Whashton, 3 miles from Richmond, T01784-822884, www.whashtonsprings.co.uk. B&B in a 17th-century farmhouse with superb views over Swaledale.

££ Willance House, 24 Bridge St, T01748-824467, www.williancehouse.com. Dating from the 17th-century, this is a great little guesthouse in a central location, but only has 3 rooms. Free Wi-Fi and a fantastic breakfast.

Restaurants

Ilkley *p94*
£££ Box Tree Restaurant, 35-37 Church St, T01943-608484, www.theboxtree.co.uk. Closed Mon. The French-style food and wine are exceptional, as you'd expect at a Michelin-starred restaurant, one of only a few in Yorkshire. Worth treating yourself for.

Skipton *p95*
££ Bull at Broughton, 4 miles west of Skipton, T01756-792065, www.thebullat broughton.com. Village pub overlooking the Broughton Hall Estate. The hearty pub fare is locally sourced as much as possible.
££ Le Caveau, 86 High St, T01756-794274, www.lecaveau.co.uk. Closed Sun-Mon. One of the best options, with modern European cooking in an elegant atmosphere.
££-£ Woolly Sheep Inn, 38 Sheep St, T01756-700966, www.woollysheepinn.co.uk. Good selection of beer and great pub food, using local produce.
£ Bizzie Lizzies, Swadford St, T01756-701131, www.bizzielizzies.co.uk. Award-winning chippie by the canal. Locals swear these are the best fish and chips in town.

Harrogate *p100*
You can't swing a cat without hitting a restaurant, pub or teahouse in Harrogate.
£££-££ Van Zeller, 8 Montpellier St, T01423-508762, www.vanzellerrestaurants.co.uk. Closed Sun evening and Mon. Fine dining at this award-winning restaurant in the swish Montpellier area.
££ Drum and Monkey, 5 Montpellier Gardens, T01423-502650, www.drumand monkey.co.uk. Closed Sun. This seafood

restaurant in a former Victorian pub has been providing outstanding fish dishes for years.
££ Mirabelle, T01423-565551, www.mirabelle restaurant.co.uk. French cuisine using Yorkshire ingredients served in a friendly, unpretentious atmosphere. Brilliant value set menu (**£**) Mon-Thu.
£ Weeton's Deli and Café, West Park, T01423-507100, www.weetons.com. Good place to stock up on goodies for a picnic, or sample stuff here in the café, overlooking the Stray.

Richmond *p105*
££ Frenchgate, 56-61 Frenchgate, T01748-822087, www.thefrenchgate.co.uk. Open fires, colourful artwork by local artists hanging on the walls and a charming walled garden make this a top choice for lunch or dinner.
£ George and Dragon, Hudswell, T01748-518373, www.georgeanddragon hudswell.com. A few miles out of town, this village-owned pub is worth a visit for its cask ales, locally sourced food and great views from its outdoor terrace.

Transport

Skipton *p95*
Trains
Skipton is a transport hub in the South Dales, so there are services to **Leeds** (45 mins) and **Bradford** (40 mins), among other destinations.

Harrogate *p100*
Bus
National Express, www.national express.com, have services to **London** (5 hrs 20 mins) and **Leeds** (35 mins direct).

Train
Regular trains to **Leeds** (35 mins), **York** (30 mins) and **Ripon** (30 mins).

Contents

Footnotes

Index

Titles available in the Footprint *Focus* range

For the latest books, e-books and a wealth of travel information, visit us at: www.footprinttravelguides.com.

Join us on facebook for the latest travel news, product releases, offers and amazing competitions: www.facebook.com/footprintbooks.